CHRISTOPHER A. CRANE & LLOYD REEB
Foreword by Dave Blanchard, CEO, Praxis Labs

THE SOCIAL ENTREPRENEUR

Seasoned Advice to Multiply Your Impact 100x

The Social Entrepreneur: Seasoned Advice to Multiply Your Impact 100x
Copyright © 2022 by Christopher A. Crane

Requests for information should be sent via email to info@ardentmentoring.org. Visit ardentmentoring.org for contact information.

All Scripture quotations, unless otherwise indicated, are taken from the Holy Bible, New International Version®, NIV®. Copyright © 1973, 1978, 1984, 2011 by Biblica, Inc.® Used by permission of Zondervan. All rights reserved worldwide. www.zondervan.com. The "NIV" and "New International Version" are trademarks registered in the United States Patent and Trademark Office by Biblica, Inc.®

Scripture quotations marked MSG are taken from THE MESSAGE. Copyright © 1993, 2002, 2018 by Eugene H. Peterson. Used by permission of NavPress. All rights reserved. Represented by Tyndale House Publishers, a Division of Tyndale House Ministries.

Scripture quotations marked NLT are taken from the Holy Bible, New Living Translation. Copyright © 1996, 2004, 2015 by Tyndale House Foundation. Used by permission of Tyndale House Ministries, Carol Stream, Illinois 60188. All rights reserved.

Scripture quotations marked TLB are taken from The Living Bible. Copyright © 1971. Used by permission of Tyndale House Publishers, a Division of Tyndale House Ministries, Carol Stream, Illinois 60188. All rights reserved.

Scripture quotations marked NKJV are taken from the New King James Version®. Copyright © 1982 by Thomas Nelson. Used by permission. All rights reserved.

Scripture quotations marked KJV are taken from the King James Version. Public domain.

All emphases in Scripture quotations and other quotations are the author's.

Any internet addresses (websites, blogs, etc.) in this book are offered as a resource. They are not intended in any way to be or imply an endorsement by the authors; nor do the authors vouch for the content of these sites and contact numbers for the life of this book.

All rights reserved. No part of this book, including icons and images, may be reproduced in any manner without prior written permission from the copyright holder, except where noted in the text and in the case of brief quotations embodied in critical articles and reviews.

ISBN #979-8-9867645-0-4 (Paperback)
ISBN #979-8-9867645-2-8 (Kindle)
ISBN #979-8-9867645-1-1 (ePub)

Cover and interior design: YouPublish (youpublish.com)

Every entrepreneur needs key people in their life who inspire them, provide memorable and applicable advice, and relentlessly encourage them about the value of their work. For me, Chris Crane has checked all these boxes, and it is a privilege to endorse *The Social Entrepreneur* from a very personal lens. The authors help you shape a comprehensive plan—one that considers self, family, team, and mission—and most importantly, ask you to consider the direction of the Holy Spirit in your life.

Dave Blanchard, CEO and cofounder of Praxislabs.org

Chris Crane mentored me for over ten years, and I benefited significantly from the experience. In this book, Chris and Lloyd Reeb share their most important ideas to help you rapidly scale your Christian social enterprise. If you are eager to impact more lives, I highly recommend this book!

Peter Greer, president and CEO, HOPE International, and coauthor of *Mission Drift*

The Social Entrepreneur serves as a compass and a road map for those called to make a difference. As social and business entrepreneurs themselves, Chris Crane and Lloyd Reeb bring decades of wisdom for accelerating and multiplying kingdom impact. They provide a complete guide to help you do the same. If you desire to see 100x sustainable, transformational impact through your enterprise, this book is a must read.

Jim Stollberg and Tom McGehee, co-executive directors, Halftime Institute

I have known Chris Crane and Lloyd Reeb for over twenty-five years. They bring gifts of experience and wisdom to help develop and grow great social enterprises. When you read *The Social Entrepreneur* and apply its principles, you will benefit more people than you can imagine.

Ken Blanchard, coauthor of *The One Minute Manager®* and *Simple Truths of Leadership*

Dedication by Chris and Lloyd

To our mutual mentor, the late Bob Buford, our thanks for guiding us along the path of social entrepreneurship, greater joy, and fruitfulness in our lives.

Dedication by Chris

To Merrill J. Oster, Stephen O. James, and Rod Dammeyer, thank you for your wise advice to make the most of opportunities and avoid pitfalls.

Dedication by Lloyd

To my dad, Ralph A. Reeb Sr., my very earliest mentor, who not only taught us character and business but also timeless wisdom from the ancient Scriptures.

"Still other seed fell on good soil. It came up, grew and produced a crop, some multiplying thirty, some sixty, some a hundred times."

Mark 4:8

CONTENTS

Foreword by Dave Blanchard 11

Introduction 15

PART 1: THE SOCIAL ENTREPRENEUR

1. The Case for Gospel-Centered Social Entrepreneurship..... 19
2. A Social Entrepreneur's Self-Assessment......................... 31
3. Our Journeys in Social Entrepreneurship......................... 51
4. Becoming a Chief Life Officer: The Pursuit of Intentionality Without Insisting on Control 67
5. Gaining 100x Yield: Exponential Impact 79

PART 2: THE SOCIAL ENTREPRENEUR'S TEAM

6. Building a World-Class Team on Startup Funding.............. 89
7. Building a High-Performance Board................................ 105
8. Being a Transformational Social Entrepreneur.................. 113
9. Staying True to Mission... 123

PART 3: ADVICE FOR BEING A SUCCESSFUL SOCIAL ENTREPRENEUR

10. Effective Fundraising 135
11. Choosing and Using Great Mentors 145
12. Managing Through a Crisis... 155
13. Partnerships, Deals, Mergers, and Acquisitions............... 167
14. Avoiding Pitfalls... 175

15. Wise Decision-Making 185
16. Crane's Pivotal Principles of Social Entrepreneurship 199

Conclusion: The Way Forward 207

Appendices 211

Notes 215

About the Authors 221

List of Resources 223

FOREWORD

EVERY ENTREPRENEUR NEEDS key people in their life who inspire them, provide memorable and applicable advice, and relentlessly encourage them about the value of their work. For me, Chris Crane has checked all these boxes, and it is a privilege to endorse *The Social Entrepreneur* from a very personal lens. From the moment I met him on a discovery trip with microfinance pioneer Opportunity International in 2006, to the ten-plus years he has mentored the Christian entrepreneurs we serve at Praxis, to the countless times Chris has told me that our work is so valuable because of its compounding effect on entrepreneurs and those they serve, I have gotten a jolt of energy from Chris's infectious enthusiasm for the work of God in founders, builders, and ventures in the world. You will get a taste of this enthusiasm in the book he's written with his dear friend and leader of leaders, Lloyd Reeb.

You'll also find this to be a guidebook on how to be more than just a leader or an entrepreneur: what we, at Praxis, like to call a redemptive entrepreneur. What is redemptive entrepreneurship? It is the hard but worthy work of following the pattern of creative restoration through sacrifice in our life and work. That is, creating with the knowledge that we are made in the image of our creator God, and then joining Him in making all things new, and ultimately doing this all for His glory on behalf of others. If you are reading this as a Christian, perhaps you are familiar with these general ideas from the Scriptures—but it is worth stopping to note how completely countercultural these narratives are to today's entrepreneurship scene.

By and large, we are much more likely to celebrate the creator than the Creator, much more likely to choose profit over purpose. We are used to the Exploitative Way, to gain any advantage, to prevail, to win the spoils. Exploitative actors often approach the venture with a zero-sum "I win, you lose" mentality. The motivating force behind the Exploitative Way is fundamentally self- or tribe-centered—to win and control. Of course, even in the work of social entrepreneurship we often see an underlying motive of self-elevation that truncates how much (if anything) we are willing to sacrifice for the good of others. We are surrounded by the Exploitative Way, we all fall naturally into it, and we are always trying to escape its effects on ourselves.

The Ethical Way is another path widely accepted as the maximal reasonable expectation of the individual or corporation. After all, the narrative goes, "We are here to succeed. But let us do that while being noble as we 'do things right'—doing no harm, keeping the rules, playing fair, solving problems, and adding value." Ethical actors pursue "win-win" whenever they can. The motivating force behind the Ethical Way is to be good and do good, which can often also be self- or tribe-centered. This is, by and large, good. We expect the Ethical Way of ourselves and of those around us, and we are grateful when we encounter it, yet we sometimes fall short.

But there is more for us here, modeled in the life of Jesus. The Redemptive Way pursues the idea, as the authors write, that the gospel is the answer to everything. Through our work as entrepreneurs, we can truly bless others, take part in the renewal of culture, and die to self so others can flourish. Redemptive actors pursue a "when I sacrifice, we all win" approach with the agency and resources available to them. The motivating force behind the Redemptive Way is fundamentally other-centered: to love and serve. This is both the countercultural struggle and the meaningful opportunity to live out our faith in action. While society rarely expects to encounter the Redemptive Way, whenever we do, we're changed.

Of course, it can also be just as likely that in our vocations we embrace the status quo, the reliable job, the standard paycheck—knowing there is risk for us to take, but often we are not willing to take it.

But entrepreneurship directs our agency and resources toward organizational creation, innovation, and risk, and Chris and Lloyd will help you understand this, understanding whether you are truly a founder, and if this is the time for you to take on this next assignment from the Lord. The authors are mindful of considering a comprehensive plan—one that considers self, family, team, and mission—and most importantly, asks you to consider the direction of the Holy Spirit in your life.

This journey from the exploitative to the ethical to the redemptive, which is both linear and daily at times, is the path from pure self-interested success to the meaningful life of significance—a journey both of your authors have taken themselves as well as guided hundreds of others on. I trust that you'll benefit from their accumulated wisdom as you seek this life of meaningful risk and holy adventure for yourself.

— Dave Blanchard, CEO and cofounder of Praxis, praxislabs.org

INTRODUCTION

SOCIAL ENTREPRENEURS TRANSFORM the lives of hundreds of millions of people, combining creative ideas with compassionate hearts, using their unique abilities to turn ideas into action. Their work might involve microfinance programs that help disadvantaged people work their way out of poverty or provide justice to widows in Africa by protecting them from forced marriages and having their homes taken away. Some are multiplying financially sustainable healthcare clinics to provide medical services and pharmaceuticals in emerging nations to people who otherwise would not be able to access them. Others help propel the growth of low-fee, financially sustainable independent schools that offer quality education at affordable prices to children of the working poor. One social entrepreneur we have mentored has grown a call center business employing more than five hundred visually impaired adults who have found both meaning and community in this friendly work environment. By building houses, drilling wells, or championing a myriad of other enterprises for disadvantaged persons, these leaders dramatically change people's lives economically, socially, physically, educationally, and sometimes, spiritually.

The world needs more social entrepreneurs. Billions of additional people's lives can be transformed through innovative social enterprises founded upon the tried-and-true principles in this book. We encourage you to start on your own social entrepreneur journey and know the profound joy of helping people change their lives for the better.

Although Chris and Lloyd each have more than twenty years of social entrepreneur experience and incorporate their Christian faith into their work, this book contains important advice for any social entrepreneur. If you are not coming from a faith perspective, we hope you will not be put off by references to the Bible and Jesus, but rather use our advice to greatly multiply the number of people you impact whether you share our faith or not.

You can also access many resources mentioned in this book at our portal website, thesocialentrepreneur.org/tools, and through Ardent Mentoring, which Chris and Lloyd cofounded with Ryan King and Steve Soars in 2021 as a community of Christian mentors to serve qualified social entrepreneurs of any faith or no faith. Ardent Mentoring considers the stage of your organization, track record, vision, strategy, revenue, and staff level and seeks to match you with a mentor with the proper expertise.

Part 1 of the book is all about you and enhancing your abilities as an entrepreneur. Part 2 is about building a world-class team on a start-up budget, and Part 3 contains detailed, practical advice on the most critical issues you will face as an entrepreneur.

At thesocialentrepreneur.org/tools, you can download the "100x Social Entrepreneur Road Map"—an Excel template for you not only to capture your most valuable learning from this book but also to create simple action steps. You can build a one-page plan for your success.

PART 1

THE SOCIAL ENTREPRENEUR

1

THE CASE FOR GOSPEL-CENTERED SOCIAL ENTREPRENEURSHIP

SEAN AND JANET Lambert are social entrepreneurs who cofounded Youth With A Mission (YWAM) San Diego/Baja in 1991. Their mission was to share the gospel and build small homes just south of Tijuana for impoverished families living in terrible conditions—in shacks with leaky roofs and dirt floors that cause everything and everyone to become wet and muddy when it rains. The roofs are often blue plastic tarps that collapse into the house if enough rain falls. In that area, three to six children often live with their parent(s). Sickness is very common. The new small homes, about the size of a two-car garage in a typical American home, are life-transforming for the recipients.

After building two hundred homes, Sean phoned Chris for advice, sounding very stressed. He was seriously thinking about quitting. His enterprise was out of money. Hard pressed, Sean had been covering the negative cash flow from operations by charging a large amount of ministry expenses on his personal credit cards, which were now far overextended. The ministry would likely close its doors. Sean was losing sleep while worrying and searching for solutions.

This news saddened me. My wife and I loved Sean and Janet and the trips we had made with them with our son to build homes. I asked basic economic questions regarding supply and demand. Sean explained that he had no shortage of excited church groups willing to pay to come build homes. He was operating at full capacity, sometimes turning away groups or having to schedule them far into the future. Sean said, "My holy grail is low prices and great service." I asked if any group ever said the prices were too high. Sean proudly said no because his prices were much lower compared to other ministries building homes with groups.

My nearly twenty years of experience as an entrepreneur had taught me that losing money when you have more demand than you can handle means your prices are too low. I recommended that Sean immediately increase his prices by 50 percent and then in twelve months increase them by an additional 50 percent. Sean was very reluctant; he was afraid that higher prices would disappoint builder groups and they would stop coming. But I said, "If you do not raise prices, in a few months you will be out of business, and then everyone will be disappointed." Worse, many poor families would never receive a home.

> "IN A FEW MONTHS YOU WILL BE OUT OF BUSINESS, AND THEN EVERYONE WILL BE DISAPPOINTED."

After our conversation, Sean did some cost accounting and found he was charging far less than even his variable costs. He lost money on every house! He took the advice to charge more, and groups kept coming, as many as he could handle. Soon the enterprise had positive cash flow to pay off debt and reinvest to make the homes better for those receiving them and offer attractive new features for builder groups. He was now able to accommodate more staff to accommodate more groups to come and build even more homes for the poor.

Later, I brought my company employees to build homes with Sean, and I encouraged friends who owned companies to do the same. Employees were so moved by the experience that I helped organize annual groups consisting of twenty business owners and sixty of their family members to come and build. Many of those CEOs then brought teams of their employees to build for multiple years. These company groups were willing to pay even higher prices for better accommodations and food.

Eventually I encouraged Sean to form a board of directors made up of both ministry leaders and business leaders. I became the first chairman. Several of the CEOs with strong governance experience, who had built homes for the poor, were willing to serve on the board.

Through the diligent and heroic efforts of Janet and Sean Lambert and their now 220 full-time staff, YWAM San Diego/Baja in 30 years has built over 7500 homes for impoverished families in 24 countries. All these families have the gospel explained to them in a culturally sensitive manner and are given a chance to receive Jesus. Tens of thousands of Americans, Canadians, Germans, Norwegians, and other nationalities have volunteered their labor and paid for building materials to construct homes. YWAM now owns property totaling 18 acres in Tijuana and Ensenada, from which more than 20 YWAM ministries serve the material, social, educational, emotional, and spiritual needs of disadvantaged families. Donors, almost all businesspeople who have built homes with YWAM, have funded approximately $20 million of buildings, all of which are debt-free. Most of those buildings accommodate staff and builder groups. Sean says that without the trajectory-changing advice on the phone call with Chris, he would have quit, and thousands of families never would have received homes.

That is what 100x social entrepreneurship advice looks like. In Mark 4:20 Jesus told a story about a farmer planting seed, and some of the seed fell on various kinds of poor soil that did not produce a crop. He likened us to soil into which He planted seeds of His grace and mercy. Then Jesus shared His vision that our lives could be extraordinary soil: "Others, like seed sown on *good soil*, hear the word, accept it, and produce a crop—some thirty, some sixty, some a hundred times what was sown." So Jesus gave us the exciting vision that our lives could be the soil through which He produces thirty, sixty, or a hundredfold.

Sean says he is already at 30x, and he continues building an increasing number of homes for the poor every year. He will pass 100x during his lifetime. In the same way that the Lord gave me the privilege of advising Sean, we desire to help you move to 30x or 60x or 100x impact.

DEFINITION OF SOCIAL ENTREPRENEUR

We believe thousands of talented Christian leaders desire to use their talent, education, and passion to build new, innovative enterprises that run with the effectiveness of a business for the purpose of ministry. These leaders are social entrepreneurs. In addition to having been longtime for-profit entrepreneurs, each of us has been a social entrepreneur for more than twenty years. We have learned the nuances of how marketplace principles play out in the social sector to create sustainable, efficient enterprises that scale.

Defining terms early is always helpful. Two experts in the field offer good definitions:

> "Social entrepreneurship addresses social problems or needs that are unmet by private markets or governments."[1]
>
> "Social enterprises are private organizations dedicated to solving social problems, serving the disadvantaged, and providing socially important goods that were not, in their judgment, adequately provided by public agencies or private markets."[2]

Our definition, based on our personal experience, our research, and those we have mentored, is:

> Social entrepreneurship is the work of using free market principles to address human needs (physical, emotional, social, educational, and spiritual) in innovative, scalable ways that exceed the impact a traditional nonprofit or for-profit or government agency can or would achieve. A social entrepreneur is an impassioned individual dedicated to serving disadvantaged people with long-term, often financially sustainable, solutions.

These people use their entrepreneurial skills and experience to balance revenue and expenses with their desired human transformation to maximize the long-term impact. Further, Christian social entrepreneurs expand the definition to sharing the good news of Jesus Christ in a culturally sensitive manner whenever they reasonably can in their work. These are great aims, but the first challenge social entrepreneurs face, we've found, is gaining seasoned, readily accessible advice for the unique challenges and decisions they face as they start and scale their enterprises.

MENTORING CAN MULTIPLY YOUR IMPACT IMMENSELY!

The great joy of mentoring Sean and many others demonstrates that mentoring makes a huge difference in the long-term effectiveness of Christian social entrepreneurs. Social entrepreneurs have great enthusiasm and big visions, but they often lack the expertise to make the most of their opportunities. Mentors add that expertise.

In addition to offering advice, mentors open doors among their contacts to allow social entrepreneurs to scale much more rapidly than they would otherwise. Mentoring helps social entrepreneurs transform 5x, 10x, and even 100x more lives.

We hope this book blesses you so you can bless many others by increasing your impact in a similar way. We offer advice for those critical decision-making junctures and inflection points. These are the times when making good decisions will make the most of big opportunities. And we want to help you avoid the many pitfalls that can set your progress back years or even sink you. The advice in this book and the resources to which we link (at the end of the book), combined with our team of seasoned mentors, will help you multiply your impact by leveraging your unique style of entrepreneurial leadership and aligning with the power of the gospel.

LEGAL STRUCTURE

A social enterprise can be for profit, not-for-profit, or an L3C (low profit, limited liability corporation); it also may be large or small, local, national, or global. It generally serves significantly disadvantaged people. Regardless of the organization's structure, some key success factors are essential to get right. Beginning with the most important ingredient, which is you—the entrepreneurial leader.

LEVERAGE

If you want to be the soil that produces a hundredfold, and change the world in a lasting way, you must find ways to gain leverage; in other words, you must bring in resources that allow you to accomplish far more than you ever could on your own. "Enterprise leverage" is an offshoot of the traditional definition of "leverage"—the mechanical advantage or power gained by using a lever. "Enterprise leverage" is the power to act or to influence people, events, and decisions. In business we leverage banks' and investors' money to make more money than we could using just our own money. We leverage the talent of our employees to produce value that exceeds what we could produce on our own.

We believe *entrepreneurial leadership* is where leverage is maximized. If you feel called as an entrepreneur to use that ability to change the world, rather than primarily for your own benefit, we believe your leadership is key to multiplying impact.

That being said, the gospel is the most powerful leverage for transforming lives. Few things in this world last, so imagine if you could invest your life in something that was guaranteed to last. Gospel-centered entrepreneurial leadership will align your work with the power of the Spirit of God, which will produce lasting results when everything else around you is temporary. This is exactly what Paul prayed would happen in the lives of the leaders he addressed in 2 Thessalonians 1:11–12: "[We] pray that our God will make you fit for what he's called you to be, pray that he'll fill your good ideas and acts of faith with his own energy so that it all amounts to something" (MSG). When your best ideas and courageous entrepreneurial efforts are empowered by the Spirit of God, imagine what the eternal results will be.

Isn't that what we all want? We want to know our work and our lives made an impact that outlasted us, or at least "amounts to something." We believe long-lasting and profound transformation involves helping people discover a relationship with Jesus Christ. We may play one small role in their journey, show compassion, model Jesus, or make the message come alive for them. When we center our lives and work around encouraging others toward Christ, we move toward making an eternal impact.

THE KEY TO LEVERAGING TRANSFORMATION

Our friend and mentor Bob Buford, a successful social entrepreneur and the author of the book *Halftime*, taught us that the entrepreneurial-style leader is where leverage *begins*. Bob is a great example of someone who invested his time, social capital, and money in such a way as to produce 100x impact in other people's lives. "Life change" was his measure. But to get 100x return on life, he needed leverage.

> "THE ENTREPRENEURIAL-STYLE LEADER IS WHERE LEVERAGE BEGINS."
> – BOB BUFORD

Peter Drucker, perhaps the greatest author ever on management, was a mentor to Bob over many years, and he turned Bob's attention toward investing in entrepreneurs. Specifically, Drucker championed a new kind of entrepreneur, the social entrepreneur, and challenged Bob to find and inspire such people. This is an excerpt from what Peter Drucker wrote to Bob in January of 1989 at the start of Bob's social entrepreneurship adventure:

> The reason you are important, Bob, is not that you have money. The reason is that you have thought through an entrepreneurial

> role. You are a pioneer. You are establishing something terribly important, and that is a NEW form of entrepreneurship that is focused on the contribution of the individual, not on the contribution of money.

Bob experienced firsthand Peter Drucker's willingness to "invest" in him because he was an entrepreneurial leader. Bob believed you should invest in the leader first and the strategy second. If you get the right leader, then the leader will fix the strategy.

> INVEST IN THE LEADER FIRST AND THE STRATEGY SECOND.

Entrepreneurs are often driven by an opportunity they believe they must pursue. They are willing to take risks that most of us avoid. Innovations have great growth potential but almost always require an entrepreneur to blossom. Bob looked for talented social entrepreneurs, people focused passionately on helping others as well as achieving financial sustainability, who wanted to bring God's blessings to others for four reasons. We believe these four reasons are instructive for all entrepreneurial leaders:

1. They are willing to risk money, time, and their reputation on ideas that have high potential of return.
2. They have the essential ability to cast the vision, build and inspire a team, and garner momentum.
3. They don't require that all the answers, systems, or processes are in place before they get started.
4. They will persevere through those inevitable times when their venture is on the brink of failure. They will power through when others abandon them; when peers, experts, and those they serve are critical of them; when misguided governments or ill-willed people attempt to shut down their operations; and when they encounter virtually every other intimidating obstacle.

If you have the above four attributes, you have the potential to be a social entrepreneur who will impact millions of lives!

Not everyone is wired to be an entrepreneur. Strong professional managers are great assets and invaluable to entrepreneurs, but Bob believed entrepreneurs are where leverage *begins*. Before Bob went to heaven in 2019, Lloyd partnered with him for more than twenty years in founding and growing what today is the global movement known as the Halftime Institute. In addition, Bob was instrumental in the creation of the Drucker Institute. These social movements he started still impact a compounding number of people around the world. Thus, Bob's impact continues. Bob was primarily motivated by the teachings of Jesus, as are we. That said, if you are not a Jesus follower, we applaud your desire to give back and hope you will draw from this book as much value as possible while taking our faith language in stride.

STAYING GOSPEL-CENTERED WITHOUT BEING OBNOXIOUS

If your work is going to have lasting, profound impact beyond just this life, it must be gospel-centered. Because all the grace that flows through us to bless others comes from the gospel—that is where the power is. But that doesn't mean your organization needs to communicate the central message of the gospel at every turn. That would be unwise and counterproductive. On the other hand, you miss an important eternal opportunity if you think, *We are doing good things to help people, so it is okay if we never share the message of God's love and forgiveness through Jesus.* Your challenge as the leader is to find the best balance for your unique calling and mission.

We believe to remain gospel-centered means:

You and your team operate from the central belief that Jesus' death for our sins and resurrection is good news and that He is the only source of living hope for everyone you serve.

Gospel-centered social entrepreneurship is about building a countercultural organization for the common good. On the surface your organization might look much like any compassionate or cause-driven service organization, but the core of it must be firmly grounded in the truth that the only hope for mankind is the cross of Jesus, His resurrection, salvation through grace, and His love for us. That Jesus is the ultimate answer to everyone's pain and emptiness is a belief we live out daily as social entrepreneurs.

As Tim Keller teaches, the gospel is the good news, and it is historical, factual, and not just good advice for living a better life. Tim defines it this way: "There's a big difference between advice and news. . . . Advice is counsel about something to do, and it hasn't happened yet, but you can do it. . . . News is a report about something that has happened. You can't do anything about [it]. It's been done for you, and all you can do is respond to it."[3] So gospel-centered work is rooted in something that has already been done for the world. It's not something you have to fight for because it's already done.

Also, the gospel is not about laws and regulations. Followers of Jesus are messengers, not advisors. If we are truly gospel-centered, then through our work our community will know we love them and that we genuinely seek the welfare of those we serve. The broader community may dislike our views on family, sexuality, and an ultimate truth source, but they will love how we bring openhanded compassion, healing, education, and financial help to those in need.

The gospel is the core solution to every problem. Hebrews 13:21 says He will "equip you with all you need for doing his will. May he produce in you, through the power of Jesus Christ, every good thing" (NLT). People struggle to transform their own lives, but the good news of the gospel is transformational.

GOSPEL + ENTREPRENEURSHIP = ETERNAL IMPACT

As social entrepreneurs, we move into the pain and despair of this world with hope for eternity. We may or may not be celebrated for our good works in this life, and we even could be persecuted for our core belief that the only real hope for people is the gospel. Yet the Bible challenges us to work in such a way that our culture sees our good deeds and glorifies God. We are strangers in the world, sojourners—not tourists or citizens. We seek the welfare of the community, but we share the good news as historic truth, not mere advice.

While some will always object to the gospel, we offer no benefit by being overbearing. Being a gospel-centered social entrepreneur is to bring God's love and grace to the deepest needs in our world in effective ways that make the work sustainable, sharing the good news of God's love and sacrifice in winsome ways. And there are many creative ways to go about this as well as many kinds of social entrepreneurs. So let's begin with who you are.

2

A SOCIAL ENTREPRENEUR'S SELF-ASSESSMENT

THE MOST IMPORTANT question to begin with is: Are you an entrepreneur and if so, what kind of entrepreneur are you?

Tim Sittema is a real estate developer in Charlotte, North Carolina, who came through the Halftime Institute in a peer group that Lloyd led. Through the yearlong roundtable, Tim realized that his calling was to stay in his business and use his expertise and influence to build a social enterprise to provide affordable housing and related essential services to one of the most disadvantaged communities in the city.

Using his credibility as a successful real estate developer, Tim built a team of accomplished peers. Working together, they formulated a creative, agile strategy that focused on only one geographic area of Charlotte, at the confluence of housing, education, employment, and health and wellness.

Tim is still leading a large, successful development firm that is growing rapidly—so he must gain the leverage of high-capacity peers who have expertise, wisdom, connections, and wealth. He leverages programs that are already working in the community as well as finding and promoting local, talented leaders in the community. Most of the time he stays in the background.

Tim told us:

> What really captured my heart is that research shows that 90 percent of a child's brain is developed by age 5. Research also shows that providing quality early education translates into long-term education and economic success. As we began our work in the Freedom Drive Corridor, we discovered the area was considered a "childcare desert" for 4- and 5-star early education for children aged 0 to 3, which puts the community at a significant disadvantage when it comes to the future potential of its children.

Among all his projects, the one that really grabs Tim's heart is the Tuck Opportunity Hub. It is a perfect example of how his life has produced a 100x impact. It's a WIN-WIN-WIN! According to Tim:

- They preserved a historic building and brightened up the community.
- They partnered with a trusted community leader and helped her expand her childcare business and added fifteen new jobs.
- They worked with stakeholders and responded to educational crises in a way that met one of the community's greatest needs.
- They pushed forward on their larger goal of equipping the next generation of neighborhood children with a strong educational foundation.
- They included their friends, which left an impact on those families.

Tim's effectiveness comes from knowing he is strong in vision, strategy, and influence. In what ways might a deeper understanding of your unique strengths and experiences help you make your biggest impact?

Not all leaders are entrepreneurs, and not all entrepreneurs are the same. The impact of an organization flows from its leadership; thus, building a social enterprise that will have exponential impact begins with you. So much of the organizational design, values, and team makeup flow from a deep personal assessment of your leadership style, gifts, and flaws.

Also, the "why" behind your enterprise is the essential foundation for your enterprise. If you are not clear on why this organization exists or do not have deep passion to grow it, you will not likely stick with it through the tough times ahead. And the reason for your existence won't be clear to the team or your customers. Make sure to be very clear on your "why."

> NOT ALL LEADERS ARE ENTREPRENEURS, AND NOT ALL ENTREPRENEURS ARE THE SAME.

WHERE TO BEGIN

The temptation is to jump right into strategy by addressing important questions such as: What business are you in? Who is your customer? What does your customer value? Whom do you need on the team to make the impact you desire?

Instead, we suggest that you begin by giving careful thought to five foundational questions about yourself—and from that understanding design the organization. These questions are a form of self-assessment that is vital for the entrepreneurial leader:

1. Are you really an entrepreneur? If so, what kind of entrepreneur are you?
2. What are your personal long-term metrics?
3. What are your primary strengths and expertise (and weaknesses), and how can you distill those qualities into a few words so your contribution is clear to the stakeholders?
4. What is your personal mission statement or calling?
5. What will be your best role in the organization after it has gained shape and momentum?

We are going to provide you a simple, proven framework to begin answering each of these questions for yourself. Then we suggest you share them with those who know you best and get their feedback. Let's unpack these questions one by one.

1. *Are you really an entrepreneur? If so, what kind of entrepreneur are you?* We like how Dictionary.com defines an entrepreneur: "a person who organizes and manages any enterprise, especially a business, usually with considerable initiative and risk."[4] "Entrepreneur" comes from an old French word *entreprendre*, which French economist Jean-Baptiste Say described as one who "shifts economic resources out of an area of lower and into an area of higher productivity and greater yield."[5]

- What evidence can you point to that shows you have entrepreneurial skills?
- Have you identified a need and created something to fill it?
- Have you shown that you can turn an idea into a simple plan and convince others to join in?
- Entrepreneurship always involves embracing uncertainty. Have you taken personal risks to make new things come to be?
- Are you sufficiently excited and committed to jump into this new enterprise by leaving your job or forgoing other opportunities, spending much of your own money and time to get started, and being willing to risk losing that money as well as appearing to be a failure in the eyes of others?
- What do your friends and colleagues say when you ask for an honest assessment of your vision?

If you answer yes to most of those questions, you're likely an entrepreneur. If not, take comfort—the Lord gives different callings. Lloyd has coached many successful corporate leaders and consultants who thrived in corporate settings but struggled and often failed when they took on an entrepreneurial role. However, some thrived as chief operating officers or other professional management roles at social enterprises, leaving the entrepreneurship to the CEO/ED. You may want to

A Social Entrepreneur's Self-Assessment

test out your idea before you jump headlong into it. Do what we call a "low-cost probe" with a "minimum viable product" or "lean startup." Test it on a small scale to see if it gains traction before leaving your current vocation.

There are different types of entrepreneurs, and knowing which one or two types best align with your personal traits will be helpful as you shape your organization. Here are a few:

- *Visionary and Inspirational Entrepreneur*: Entrusts management to professional managers.
- *Startup Entrepreneur*: Loves the challenge of starting from scratch.
- *Ramp-up Entrepreneur*: Comes to an existing social enterprise and scales it rapidly from the existing base.
- *Turnaround Entrepreneur*: Brought to a troubled social enterprise with the hope of returning it to firm footing and growth.

The Bible is also full of entrepreneurs God used to accomplish His plans in the world, and they were very different from one another:

- Moses was a stable, courageous leader who overcame rejection ten times (in the story of the ten plagues), stayed close to the Lord during forty years of leadership, persevered through rebellion both against him and against God, mentored Joshua, and led the Israelites to the point of entry into the promised land. Moses exhibited all four entrepreneur types listed above.
- Joshua was always ready to take on any challenge, moved out boldly and courageously, and "[banished] fear and doubt" (Josh. 1:9, TLB). Joshua was a ramp-up entrepreneur, building on the foundation laid by Moses.
- Deborah was the leader of Israel (Judg. 4:4) when it had been cruelly oppressed for twenty years by the king of Canaan and his general, Sisera, who had nine hundred chariots fitted with iron. She sought the Lord for a plan, chose Barak, accompanied him to the field, and directed him when and where to attack.

Under her leadership, the Israelites won a great victory. She was a turnaround entrepreneur.
- Paul responded to the Lord's call to follow and proclaim Jesus. He shared the gospel in many nations, adapting to strange customs with foreign gods and numerous imprisonments, overcoming extreme resistance of shipwrecks, five beatings of thirty-nine strokes of the rod, and much more. He said his life was "being poured out like a drink offering" (2 Tim. 4:6). Paul persevered against severe adversity because of his calling and commitment to achieve his mission. He was the startup kind of entrepreneur.

2. *What are your personal long-term metrics?* Metrics allow entrepreneurs to measure organizational success and provide guidance along the way as they allocate resources and adapt strategies. The same is true in your own life, and because you are the entrepreneur forming and leading this effort you need to be clear on your own personal metrics first.

The organization you launch or grow needs to be accretive to your long-term personal desires.

How is this organization you are investing so much time and effort into helping to create the life you want in the long run?

This is the idea of beginning with the ending in mind. Not just the desired results of the organization but also more fundamentally the life you want. Lloyd coaches a couple now who are deep into building award-winning restaurants that employ disadvantaged people. They make a difference in the lives of their employees and inspire their customers by their compassion. But the job conflicts with the family life the entrepreneurs want.

At this moment they are faced with a tough choice of following through on their dream of building the restaurants to be a sustainable social enterprise, or changing that vision by slowing the progress so they don't jeopardize priceless time with the kids while they are still at home. In our view the restaurants are valuable, but the family is priceless, and it never makes sense to trade what is priceless for what is merely valuable.

We would never build a business strategy without clear, long-term metrics describing what a win looks like. When Lloyd helped Bob Buford launch the Halftime Institute, he shared with Bob his personal goals for the next year, which were nestled inside a set of five-year goals. After listening for a while, Bob said, "Lloyd, each year you share with me these noble and well-thought-out goals, but you never tell me where they are taking you. To what end?"

His assignment to Lloyd was to spend several weeks noodling on the question, *If your life turned out perfectly, what would the elements be?* This is the question we want you to begin with. This will help you define the primary loyalties of your life.

Some of these elements may be easy to measure and some more difficult, but for the time being, just focus on the desired results for your life. We can sort out how to measure them later.

Think of it this way. Suppose we bump into each other many years from now at the very end of our lives, and we ask you how the interim years went. After deep reflection, you say, "You won't believe it, but they went perfectly." What are the factors you would have to scroll through in your mind to draw that conclusion?

Write them here:

_____

_____

_____

_____

_____

That's a start. Now we suggest that you talk these over with your family and friends to get their input and perspective. Keep refining them. If it's helpful as an example, Lloyd's long-term life metrics are to worship God every day, to become someone who gives liberally, to have a few deep, intimate relationships, to make a leveraged kingdom impact as a thought leader, to stay in tip-top shape, and to spend his life surrounded by beauty. Because the long-term metrics are so central to his life, Lloyd keeps them handy. He has carried a plasticized version in his wallet for several decades.

He pulls them out regularly and asks, "Am I living my life in alignment with these long-term desired results?" As a result, they have become a plumb line for his life and helped shape major choices. They have helped him determine how to allocate his time in the face of the exciting global growth of the Halftime Institute social enterprise.

3. *What are your primary strengths and expertise?* Peter Drucker taught that if you focus on your strengths, you make your weaknesses irrelevant. Most of us were taught to focus on bringing our C's up to B's. But the idea of strengths-based leadership is that you double down on those few things that you are naturally great at. When you do this, time flies and your tasks seem easy. It's energizing. If you have not done an in-depth assessment of your strengths, we encourage you to come at it from several different perspectives.

First, take some time to reflect on your natural gifts and talents. Next, examine your life up to this point. When were you at your best? What were the circumstances and what were you doing? What technical skills and expertise have you developed so far? You have probably taken multiple personality and aptitude tests. What did you learn from those? We also suggest that you go online and take the CliftonStrengths Assessment (formerly known as StrengthsFinder Assessment).[6]

Lloyd's top five talent themes from the CliftonStrengths Assessment are strategic, futurist, activator, belief, and focus. Thus, his strengths can be summarized in a few words: he is a thought leader. He leverages these strengths by staying out of operational leadership roles.

Instead, he focuses on thought leadership and allows others with management strengths to operate the Halftime Institute. Chris's top five talent themes in the CliftonStrengths Assessment are achiever, competitor, woo, focus, and ideation. His strengths can be summarized as a "make it happen" entrepreneur. He is a visionary and dealmaker who has succeeded by hiring professional managers. Now, at age seventy, he mentors other Christian social entrepreneurs to turn great ideas into great impact in their field.

Now try to synthesize your observations of your God-given abilities, with the top talent themes from CliftonStrengths, into three or four words that best describe your strengths. This will help you know what to focus your efforts on and what work to let others do, and you will be able to model for your team the value of working in the areas of your strengths.

4. *What is your personal mission statement or calling?* Knowing that you are living out your calling will provide staying power when times are tough or when the journey seems long. You likely already have a pretty good sense of your calling. The fact that each of us has an assignment from the Lord gives each day meaning and purpose.

Imagine the incredible meaning and staying power that John the Baptist experienced knowing he was on an assignment from God: "There was a man sent from God whose name was John. He came as a witness to testify concerning that light, so that through him all might believe" (John 1:6–8). He was named specifically, his mission clearly stated that he was to witness concerning the Light, and the desired results were that through him all might believe. That's a clear mission statement!

Now think about a similar sentence for yourself. One simple way is to insert your name and role and desired results into that same verse:

> There was a person sent from God whose name is (*your name*), who came as a (*your role*), so that (*God's desired results for your life*).

Sometimes we feel that trying to define our mission in a sentence is like telling God what we will and won't do. But it's helpful to think of it as heuristic writing, in other words, writing down what you believe you are hearing from the Lord regarding the "good works, which God prepared in advance for us to do" (Eph. 2:10).

When you write a mission statement as a form of heuristic writing, you write as a way of understanding, discovering, or listening both to your heart and to the Lord. As Eugene Peterson says, it is "writing as a way of entering into language and letting language enter me, words connecting with words and creating what had previously been inarticulate or unnoticed or hidden. . . . [w]riting as an act of prayer."[7]

For some, this feels too confining. For example, Lloyd's wife, Linda, felt her style of living was to wake up every day and do what she could to serve her family and others as needs arose. When asked about her calling, she didn't want to confine it to a written mission statement. That is, until she had a year of panic and anxiety, and she realized she couldn't keep doing everything that she was doing. She had no filter to say no to things, and it became unsustainable to raise the kids, lead a small group, work part-time, volunteer in the community, play in the church band, share the gospel with neighbors, be an engaged sister and daughter and spouse, etc., all at the same time.

> *Because she didn't have a* solid yes *in life, she didn't have a* firm no.

With some personal assessments and reflection, she discovered that her strengths are teaching and mentoring, and she is most passionate about helping young moms build healthy marriages and families—before they drift apart in their forties. It turned out that having a mission was not confining; instead, it was freeing. Now her mission is to mentor young moms so they infuse God's wisdom into their homes by building strong marriages and godly families.

This process to gain clarity about your calling is broken down into bite-sized pieces for us in Galatians 6:

> Make a careful exploration of who you are and the work you have been given, and then sink yourself into that. Don't be impressed with yourself. Don't compare yourself with others. Each of you must take responsibility for doing the creative best you can with your own life. (Gal. 6:4–5, MSG)

According to this passage from Galatians, we are to work on three tasks:

- Give careful thought to who you are: your personality, experiences, expertise, strengths, spiritual gifts, and passions. If you are not sure of your passions, you may have to broaden your exposure to the wide array of ministries in your community and the human needs around the country or world.
- Look around at the possibilities. What is God doing that aligns with your strengths and interests? How could you get exposed to a wider array of organizations? Explore other organizations online, go visit them, or have conversations with others involved in the causes you find interesting. As you explore, remember that your calling is a gift to receive, not a goal to achieve. If you don't follow your destiny, as Spanish philosopher José Ortega Gasset once wrote, it will follow you like an "accusing shadow."[8]
- Take responsibility to be creative in how to tackle that work. Specifically, this means what kind of organization will enable you to accomplish this? What role should you play in that organization(s)? Would you do better with a portfolio of roles or by focusing on just one job? What progression of career roles and responsibilities will best prepare you for achieving your mission? This is an ongoing process of adapting as the environment changes.

A useful mission statement is a filter that helps you say no to the many good things that are the enemy of the best. Your mission should state your strengths and expertise, what you are most passionate about (a cause, or people group, or a unique contribution you can make), and the difference you most want to make in this world.

A simple way to start is to fill in this sentence below based on what you know already:

> I am a (*the kind of entrepreneur you are*) social entrepreneur, building an organization focused on (*the cause you are addressing*) so that (*the desired results*).

Don't try to get it right the first time. Start with what you know and work toward what you don't yet know. So think in terms of writing it in chalk—not permanent marker, not pen, not even pencil.

Writing something on a chalkboard makes it public; it's very easy to change and sits out in the open so you can ruminate on it as you walk past it. For example, Lloyd and Linda have a big chalkboard in their country kitchen, and when they're planning a project or family trip, they often chalk it out first and leave it up there for days. Family members add ideas, and over time they gain clarity about the project or trip.

You might be tempted to only think about your mission and not write it down. But we strongly encourage you to write it down and share it and refine it. This will provide a powerful filter to help you decide what to say yes to and what to say no to.

5. *What is your best role in the organization after it has gained shape and momentum?* Would you make your best contribution as the visionary strategist, the operations director, in advocacy across the spectrum of the cause you are focused on, in funding development, etc.? In the early stages we often must play a variety of roles. If you have a decade or more of work experience, seek the Lord as to whether you are called

to be an entrepreneurial leader or a professional manager in a Christian social enterprise. Both roles are noble callings.

However, as your enterprise matures you might be able to spawn a world-class social enterprise without being the CEO/ED. In fact, if you care deeply about maximizing your impact, you might regularly ask yourself the question, *What is my best role in this season of the organization?* Lloyd asks himself this question every ten years, which provides an important mechanism for him to evolve and get out of the way of more talented partners. After cofounding and being CEO for eight years at Edify, Chris passed the CEO baton to cofounder Tiger Dawson. Although Chris had the energy and enthusiasm to continue as CEO, he believed the Lord was calling him to transition. He is so pleased he did this. Chris now sees that Tiger is taking Edify to greater heights than would have occurred if Chris had not stepped aside at that time. Now as Edify's chairman, Chris advises other CEOs/EDs to move on when the Lord prompts them, and not to hang on and hinder stepping into the next role God has for them.

Lloyd's best contribution is strategy, understanding the customer, designing the experience, and communicating the vision and message. Over the past twenty-plus years with the Halftime Institute, his role has evolved from founding partner designing the early customer experience, to being the primary spokesperson for a decade, to today focusing on replicating talented younger leaders in the movement around the world. Only briefly was he the managing partner—just long enough to find a better leader for that role.

Chris's best contribution is identifying a major problem and solution, launching an enterprise, and building a team who can scale the solution. Chris has evolved from serving twenty-five combined years as the CEO of Comps InfoSystems, a private equity-financed and eventually publicly traded company, and then two international nonprofit social enterprises, to serving Ardent Mentoring where he now mentors high-capacity Christian social entrepreneurs with visions to transform millions of lives.

Take a minute and describe what you believe your best role is now within your enterprise:

My best role is _____

_____

If you carefully answer the above five questions well, you will do the following:

- Choose the right role for yourself now and when your enterprise has scaled.
- Be more focused sooner.
- Be a better leader.
- Build a strong team with the right people in the right positions.
- Spend more time on what you do best, which will lead to better results and more joy.
- Achieve your mission and impact more people.

Having answered the five questions, let's look at coupling your findings with achieving eternal results.

THE GREAT COMMANDMENT WITH THE GREAT COMMISSION

The Great Commandment (Matt. 22:37–39) is to love God and love your neighbor, and the Great Commission (Matt. 28:18–20) is to share Jesus. Christian social entrepreneurs operate on a spectrum regarding these callings. At one end of the spectrum are those who only focus on sharing the message of Jesus and building disciples. At the other end of the spectrum are those who seek to help others with physical needs, such as food, water, health, shelter, education, jobs, peace, etc., but they do not evangelize.

In between you can find a blend of these that emphasizes helping people physically, socially, materially, and educationally, yet going beyond that to offer them the eternity-changing message of God's forgiveness and love. Followers of Jesus may receive a calling from the Lord to operate at any point on the spectrum. We recommend that you prayerfully seek the Lord, so you are aligned with His will regarding the point on the spectrum of your organization's operations.

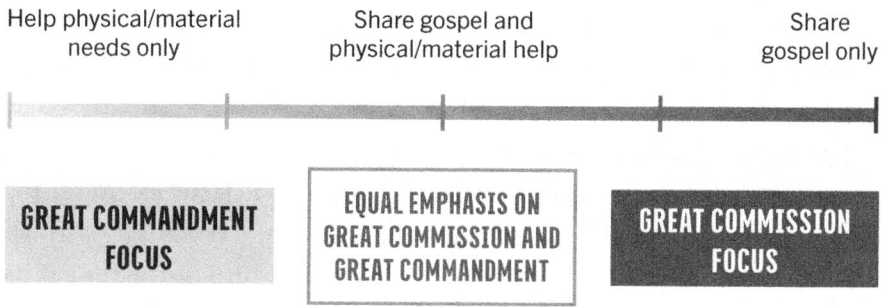

The Lord called Chris to microfinance, which emphasizes economic improvement, often accompanied by social, health, and educational improvement. However, I felt called equally to weight sharing Jesus among the activities of the organizations I managed. Having spent time with the Lord, I felt called to find creative, culturally sensitive ways my team could share Jesus' message as they earnestly sought to help people economically. I believe when I stand before Jesus, He will ask if I used the tool of microfinance to love my neighbors by helping them economically. Then He will ask, "Did you tell those people, My children, about Me?" Based on my calling, the Lord will be looking for me to say yes.

Please spend time in prayer, ideally fasting and prayer, until you have a clear leading from the Lord regarding His calling for you on this spectrum. And then embed that into the strategy and measurements for your enterprise. If your calling is both to help people and share Jesus, expect others, often well-meaning Christians, to tell you that you will broaden your fundraising base by not emphasizing Jesus in your work. They will tell you that if you openly share Jesus, many prospective donors or investors will not be interested. This is partially true; you will have some people decline to support you because you share Jesus in your work. However, over time you may raise even more money by staying true to the Great Commission. And more importantly, your organization will make a greater eternal impact.

When I became CEO of Opportunity International in 2002, it was one of the three largest USA-based microfinance organizations working in developing nations. All three organizations had similar revenues then. People suggested deemphasizing Jesus to raise more money. However, seven years later, after emphasizing the gospel message, Opportunity International's revenues were more than the other two secular organizations combined. Being open about Jesus led to raising more money than otherwise! Many donors were particularly attracted to proclaiming Jesus because of the eternal nature of the return on their donation.

Christians make up a disproportionately large percentage of giving, and many Christian philanthropists look for organizations that combine the Great Commandment with the Great Commission. We've seen in our experience that although some donors will not consider you because of your evangelical outreach, others will give more generously because of it.

If you feel called to focus primarily on the teaching of the Great Commandment to love your neighbor through material assistance, carefully frame your thinking based on biblical teachings. The Bible clearly says the treasures of earth are temporary, but unseen treasures are eternal (2 Cor. 4:18). So why would you build an organization whose intended results will disappear over time when you could focus on something that will last forever?

So what if, for example, you feel called to care for the environment? That is not directly tied to seeing people come to know Jesus. Jay Faison is a successful entrepreneur who sold his company and then went on a careful exploration of what God called him to do next. And he felt clearly led to form the ClearPath Foundation, which focuses on the environment. He uses his analytical mind and willingness to risk his capital to address some monumental challenges like flooding. After years of research and work at the ClearPath Foundation, he recently founded Flood Defenders. In his words, "I lead an organization dedicated to amplifying the voices of people impacted by flooding. Our goal is common-sense solutions at all levels of government."

With this in mind, read over the familiar verses below.

> God spoke: "Let us make human beings in our image, make them reflecting our nature so they can be responsible for the fish in the sea, the birds in the air, the cattle, and, yes, Earth itself, and every animal that moves on the face of Earth." (Gen. 1:26–28, MSG)

Jay believes he is directly living out what we are told to do in Genesis 1 by playing his part of taking responsibility for caring for this earth. Lloyd knows Jay well, and it's obvious that he is finding great fulfillment in sensing each day that he is the hands and feet of the great Creator. Jay also finds freedom in knowing God has assigned others to work in other parts of His grand plan.

OUR ADVICE

Seek the Lord as to where He is calling you to be on the Great Commandment/Great Commission spectrum. When Jesus shows you the point on the spectrum, resolve to stick with it, and ask the Lord how you can best implement the degree of emphasis to which He has called you. If you are called to emphasize the gospel, expect some to say sharing Jesus is misguided, some to close doors in your face, and some to offer large donations if you deemphasize Jesus. Keep going until you find followers of Jesus with resources who are excited about helping people while sharing Jesus.

Chris knows of two Christian international economic development organizations doing almost identical work. In 2006, the older organization had revenues twenty times greater than the younger organization, which had been founded twelve years earlier. However, the older organization started to deemphasize Jesus shortly thereafter, while the newer organization enthusiastically proclaimed Jesus in its fieldwork and fundraising. Nine years later, the revenues of the two organizations were within 10 percent of each other. Revenues for the older organization had dropped by half. Revenues at the younger organization had increased at a 28 percent compound annual growth rate.

TAKING THE EXCITING LEAP AS A SOCIAL ENTREPRENEUR

Taking the big leap and starting on your vision to change the world is exhilarating! The German poet, statesman, and philosopher Johann Wolfgang von Goethe said, "Whatever you can do or dream . . . begin it. Boldness has genius, power and magic in it."[9] You have a sense that you were designed to be an entrepreneur, you can see it in your past and in your strengths, you have a rough mission statement, and you have tested out your idea by researching what's out there and learning from those working in this space. When should you pull the trigger?

It depends on a few factors: the kind of entrepreneur you are and where you are in life.

- If you are a startup entrepreneur, do you have the business plan, cash flow pro forma, and the vision clear enough to begin attracting both talent and donors/investors to cover the costs of your launch?
- If you are a ramp-up entrepreneur or turnaround entrepreneur, have you done the hard work of researching and comparing possible organizations to ramp up or turn around? Are their boards sufficiently on your side? Do you have a clear sense of what would be needed to ramp them up or turn them around, and can you afford to invest that much effort at this season of your life? Turnarounds are a great challenge, and only a few people,

generally highly experienced in turnarounds, are suitable for the task.
- If you are a visionary/inspirational entrepreneur, is your vision clear and tested, do you have the stories and data to make it credible, and do you have the launch team in place to make the effort sustainable from the start?
- If you are young, especially if you are a college senior or have only been out of college for a few years, you may wish to get good experience in a well-run organization before beginning something yourself. There is something to be said for learning how to run a for-profit company efficiently. You will learn valuable skills to bring into social enterprise and will also have more credibility with prospective team members and donors who come from the business world. This credibility can last for your entire social enterprise career, as you will not be seen as solely a "nonprofit executive."

Both of us took this approach, and the skills and experiences we gained in our first decades of work have multiplied our impact in these last twenty-five years. We invite you to do the same. As Lloyd often told his children when they were in their twenties, "If you want to change the world, get good at something." The next chapter speaks more about our respective social entrepreneur journeys.

3

OUR JOURNEYS IN SOCIAL ENTREPRENEURSHIP

UNDERSTANDING OUR TWO unique journeys will not only provide encouragement for you in your twisting road to creating an organization that truly changes the world, but it also will help you understand how our different backgrounds provide you complementary perspectives for your journey.

LLOYD'S STORY

For me, the journey from real estate entrepreneur to social entrepreneur was the transition from how to make a living to how to make a life. I made mistakes and encountered many obstacles in the transition—ones that I hope you will avoid. I also capitalized on some big opportunities that the Lord provided, and I have been absolutely thrilled with and amazed by what I have seen God do through me. I want to help you do the same.

Smoldering Discontent. Having achieved some measure of success in my early thirties by developing real estate, I had accumulated more than we needed yet found something was still missing. My wife, Linda, and I had three young children, and we had just built our dream house on a farm in Canada overlooking the Big Rideau Lake. Life was wonderful. But I felt a smoldering discontent inside that there had to be more to life than just building one project after another and growing our net worth for me and my little family.

A Change of Perspective. I took a trip with a friend through Asia, partly for pleasure and partly to visit missionary friends. I spent a week in downtown Hong Kong enjoying the excitement and amazing food. Then I spent a week helping friends serve street children in the Philippines. I flew from Manila to a beautiful resort in Malaysia on the South China Sea. As I sat on the beach reflecting on life, I suddenly realized I found more joy helping those kids in Manila than sitting on a beach in Malaysia. The prospect of spending the rest of my life just building more buildings, accumulating more wealth, and making myself secure and comfortable was simply not enough. I wanted my life to count for something long after I was gone. I wanted to move beyond success to significance.

Slowly Finding My Niche. I sent my résumé to dozens of organizations that were addressing big areas of human suffering, but they could not see how they could use a real estate developer—even if they did not have to pay me a salary. And I did not understand how my skills could be useful to them. After several tries, I took on an executive role for a large nonprofit. Then I tried being a pastor in a large church.

But I have always been an entrepreneur, so those roles were not a good fit—as much as I loved the work they accomplished. However, that experience helped prepare me for what I am doing today, in part because I discovered that no one was creating a pathway for business leaders to find meaningful roles in the social sector. Also, I learned how nonprofits operate.

Building a Global Social Enterprise. In 1997 I met Bob Buford, who soon became my mentor. He had written a best-selling book in which he labeled this stage of life as "Halftime." Halftime is a pause in our midlife to reflect on who we are, what matters in the end, and how to redirect our time and resources for the next season. That's exactly what I had been experiencing. That's the need I had just identified. And he was already working on testing an organization (halftime.org) to help people in Halftime. It seemed natural to me to help build an enterprise that addressed an emerging human need, building a movement that was scalable and could operate like a business. I believed then, and believe more strongly now twenty-five years later, that *the most viable way to impact our world going forward will not be organizations that rely solely on donations but enterprises that deliver valuable products or services and run with market principles.*

So I have invested the last twenty-plus years in helping successful leaders who are having a hard time sorting out how to use their skills, expertise, and influence for good. These very talented people often feel alone in their journey and don't realize others have charted this course ahead of them and garnered resources, processes, tools, ideas, and models that will serve them in their journey. I want to bring the best of these resources to you, woven throughout this book.

> LEARN MORE ABOUT HALFTIME AT HALFTIMEINSTITUTE.ORG.

Incidentally, the midlife reinvention opportunity we call Halftime is not just for the super-rich or financially independent. It's more about options than affluence. Many different methods are out there to infuse significance into your life. Maybe for you it's about renegotiating with corporate America to work fewer hours so you can invest those hours in something you want to start—in parallel with your career—that will have more meaning to you.

The Joy. You will face risks and obstacles along the way (and we're going to talk about some of those), but I contend that going through life on autopilot, doing what we have always done, may seem safe and feel more secure, but we could end up missing out on the greatest adventure of life: the profound joy of helping thousands or millions of other fellow human beings.

Is there any greater thrill than loosening your grip, releasing your life for God's use, and seeing Him change the lives of others through your sacrifice?

WHAT MADE MY TRANSITION DIFFICULT?

As I said, transitioning from being a real estate entrepreneur to a social entrepreneur was very difficult. In fact, when Bob first heard my story, he looked me in the eye and said, "Perhaps God pulled you through that knothole so you could help others avoid those same mistakes." And that is what I have dedicated my life to. As I look back, I can clearly see what makes this transition difficult. I call this the "dumb tax." The cost of not knowing. I share these mostly to help you avoid paying the dumb tax.

I had no idea who I really was at the core. The first half of my career was based on opportunities and circumstances. Now I had to discover what I was truly passionate about. What was I placed on earth to do? What were my greatest talents (those few things I am outstanding at rather than merely competent)?

I was largely underexposed to the wide array of human issues or causes. For example, I had no awareness of human trafficking, or the issues contributing to multi-generational poverty, or what happens to kids when they graduate from foster care.

I was afraid of losing my identity. I found that my identity was way more wrapped up in being a "big-time" real estate developer than I ever dreamt. And in the same vein, I was addicted to the thrill of the deal, the adrenaline rush, and the risk of real estate development. I needed to go on a heart journey to a new identity and performance measure. I had to go through a kind of detox.

I had no idea how big the culture gap is between the business and the social sector. I did not know that some of the principles I had learned in business do not apply well to nonprofits. Some nonprofits are afraid of disruption from hard-nosed for-profit executives and entrepreneurs joining their staff. Nonprofit boards can function very differently, and staff expectations, motivations, and work pace can be very different in the two sectors.

If I could do this journey over, I would take considerable time getting clear on who I am and what my mission and desires are. I would take time to read, learn, and explore a wide array of issues that Jesus cares about. I would do the internal work of allowing God to reshape my identity and performance measures.

A FULFILLING PATH

Perhaps you are in your twenties and sense that you are not that interested in focusing on wealth creation but want to focus on doing something that has a tangible social impact on the world. Or you are in your forties, fifties, or older and want to use your experience and skills to transform the lives of others.

It's been twenty-five-plus years since I first became a social entrepreneur. I am sure I left lots of money on the table by not focusing on my real estate business, but because of the Halftime movement, thousands of talented leaders on almost every continent have gotten clear on their destiny and are free of the low-value pursuits holding them back so they can commit to transforming the lives of many people.

Many aspire to something noble, but I have encountered only a few who are willing to pay the costly price to do so. We are committed to being a wind at your back, bringing advice, resources, and mentoring to inspire and equip you on your way. We are making assessment tools, exercises, best practices, checklists, and advice available to you through the website associated with this book: thesocialentrepreneur.org/tools. In addition, most of the resources we reference in this book are listed at the back with individual links. Last, we cofounded a robust mentoring network with talented Christian mentors who have years of experience in the areas where you may need help (ardentmentoring.org).

CHRIS'S STORY

My journey from being a software/database entrepreneur to a social entrepreneur was the transition from building financial security for my family to helping families living in poverty build financial security as they grow in Christ. I was fifty years old when I started the transition, had sold my company two years prior, and was serving on for-profit boards as well as the board of Youth With A Mission San Diego/Baja.

I had always wanted to be a business entrepreneur, to build an exciting company and become financially independent. I gained experience at three companies that employed between three hundred and six hundred people. I had tried several entrepreneurial ventures but had not gained any traction. That is, until one day, when I spoke with a friend, Bob Beasley, who had been my Bible study leader in San Diego.

He had a business called Comps, Inc., later named Comps Info-Systems, that published detailed information about sales comparables for commercial real estate. His wife had filed for divorce and insisted on the sale of the company. I felt the Lord prompt me to pursue buying the company even though my wife, Jane, and I, then age forty, had very few resources.

Another bidder offered the exact same $1.6 million price I did, but twelve times as much cash up front. My wife and I didn't have that. But through a series of God-directed circumstances and negotiations, my creative attorney and I (and the Lord) structured a deal to buy 60 percent of the company, with my Bible study friend retaining 40 percent. I paid $135,000 in cash with $85,000, our life savings, and by borrowing $50,000 more from my father and brother. I negotiated another $125,000 in seller financing and personally guaranteed a $95,000 bank loan. The following day I received a fax from my sister (who happened to be a lawyer), asking me to sign a promissory note to my father. I suspected she was worried the business would not succeed, which would mean less of an inheritance for her and my other siblings!

While it was exciting to buy this company with $4 million in revenues, the picture was anything but rosy. The company had lost money each of the previous five years, and the CFO's projections showed it would run out of cash in three months. Worse, the commercial real estate industry in California was in the tank. Commercial property values had dropped by half; foreclosures and bankruptcies were rampant.

So why did I do the deal? What was I thinking?

I had sought the Lord earnestly in prayer and fasting, and I felt it was something He wanted me to do. As I waited on Him, I got a sense of peace about the deal.

> *God seemed to be telling me this would bring me to a new level of faith and spiritual maturity.*

I also sensed He was saying there would be great struggles—which there were.

For example, within a year, a much larger competitor cut its prices in half in an effort to drive my company out of business. One Sunday morning, I prayed and asked the Lord if I should approach that competitor and offer to sell the company if they would take over the bank loan I had personally guaranteed. God said no and helped my company survive. Another time, I saw no way to meet payroll due at the end of the week. Again, the Lord provided. Other times we almost went under, but we kept going because that was the calling.

Buying the company had been a step of faith, but it hadn't been a blind step. I did my due diligence. I asked twenty CEOs for advice; seventeen told me not to buy Comps InfoSystems. The three who had bought and sold companies were the only ones who thought the deal could make sense. A dear friend, Tom Noon, who had been a CFO in the same industry, spent a week with me helping analyze the acquisition by going through the financials and making projections. My former boss and longtime mentor, Merrill Oster, gave me great ideas. He identified five business areas I needed to concentrate on to improve cash flow. Following Merrill's advice seemed like painting by the numbers, and it worked. His mentoring was invaluable! Finally, Terry Greve and Nick Wallner, who had acquired thirty-three companies and had coauthored the book *How to Do a Leveraged Buyout*, were very helpful mentors. As the Bible says: "In the multitude of counselors there is safety"

(Prov. 11:14, NKJV). Choosing mentors with strong, relevant expertise can make all the difference!

Another source of great help and advice was my association with YPO (formerly Young Presidents' Organization). It helped me in several ways. YPO brought in speakers with excellent advice for small-company presidents. It also had a time-tested format for members to share their most pressing problems in a small group and then receive objective, wise counsel from presidents running similar-sized companies. If you ever have the chance to join YPO, or a group of Christian social entrepreneurs who give each other advice on a totally confidential basis, you'll be amazed at the good advice you receive.

Over the next few years, Comps InfoSystems expanded from four western states to fifty of the top real estate markets nationwide. We also changed from being a print-based publishing firm into an electronic database publisher. In 1997 and 1998, we started to grasp the power of the internet. We acquired thirteen companies, including one that matched brokers' listings directly with likely buyers.

By 1999, Comps InfoSystems had grown into the largest commercial real estate sales information company in the US. We had four hundred employees. We went ahead with an initial public offering. Six months after the IPO, a larger public company made an offer to purchase Comps at an attractive price. We sold the company in February 2000, six weeks before the stock market crashed. That precipitous decline in stock prices became known as the "tech wreck" or the "dot-com bubble burst." But God had allowed us to sell the company before that crash.

I was now free of management responsibilities and took time to relax and regroup. I served on boards of companies and ministries I believed in. I traveled a lot with my wife and son, who was then fourteen and loved trying out new surfing spots.

CHRISTIAN MICROFINANCE

About this time, the *Wall Street Journal* ran a front-page story on microfinance featuring Grameen Bank of Bangladesh and Professor Muhammad Yunus. Seven years later, Yunus won the Nobel Peace Prize for his work in this field. I was amazed that $100, $200, or $400 loans to people living in poverty could help them significantly grow their small businesses. And even more amazed by the fact that 98 percent of the borrowers repaid the loans!

That prompted my interest in microfinance. Shortly thereafter, a fundraiser from a large Christian microfinance organization, Opportunity International, called me. I made a donation and also offered to organize some fundraising events to introduce my friends to them. In the process I became friends with the CEO.

I never suspected that two years later I would have his job.

One day he called me. "I'm going to be moving on, and I've put your name in as a possible successor."

"Oh, Charlie, thanks for thinking of me," I said. "But I don't know anything about running a nonprofit organization or a Christian ministry. And you're headquartered in Chicago. Jane and I really like San Diego, and our son is still in high school."

"Are you interested in learning more about microfinance?" he asked. "Speaking with the recruiter would be a great way to do it."

I went through the interview process and was, to my great surprise, the unanimous choice of the board. My response was to ask for ten days to think and pray about it. As Jane and I discussed the possibility, to my great surprise she said, "Chris, your love for business and heart for the poor really relate to this job. If you don't take it, I think you'll always regret it." Then she added, "But let's stay in San Diego!"

She was wonderfully supportive through all our transitions. Purchasing Comps InfoSystems had been a big step for us; we had invested our life savings. Jane was just as supportive of my involvement with Opportunity International. She has always given me good advice and is my most valued counselor.

I was a for-profit businessman who knew next to nothing about nonprofits. But as I looked under the hood, I saw the similarities. This global nonprofit ran like a business, orchestrating loans and setting up partnerships and lending alliances. It was also in need of a turnaround, and I had a couple of those under my belt. They could use someone with my business experience. Also, my daily Scripture reading and its many commandments to serve the poor encouraged me to make the transition.

I was fifty years old when I became CEO of this international ministry in 2002. I commuted to Chicago one week a month and spent another week a month traveling to do fundraising. In addition, I traveled a few weeks internationally to visit our programs. I was gone from home about 135 overnights a year for the next seven years, which in retrospect was way too much travel.

Although the ministry had lost $2 million the year prior to my joining, it had good executives with sincere ambitions to grow rapidly to serve people living in poverty. By God's grace, during my seven years there, we increased annual donations from individuals and foundations from $8 million in my first year to $51 million in my last year. This was a compound annual growth rate of 31 percent, considered high even in the business world. By 2008 we were the world's largest faith-based microfinance organization and served 1.5 million clients in twenty-eight countries.

We had an amazing staff doing wonderful work helping millions of people. So why did I leave and tackle the difficult task of starting another ministry from scratch?

In 2006, I heard James Tooley, a delightful British professor of education, speak at a Templeton Foundation event. The conference focused on free enterprise solutions for educating the world's financially impoverished. This prompted some very good discussions. Later, I happened to be seated next to Professor Tooley, and we talked. What a divine coincidence! There I was, the CEO of a microfinance organization, and next to me was the foremost expert on an amazing new potential client segment that would be perfect for microfinance: low-fee, independent Christian schools.

When I first heard of the concept, I didn't know if any microfinance institutions (MFIs) made small- and medium-sized enterprise loans to schools. But after I heard Professor Tooley speak, I developed a vision for MFIs coming into this space. We could help schools expand to serve more students. Soon, I went to Kenya to research low-fee independent schools.

Makonen Getu, PhD, then at Opportunity International and now one of our capable executives at Edify, met me in Nairobi. He had grown up in Ethiopia as a poor shepherd boy and, through great diligence, travails, and miracles, got a primary-through-college education. He had to flee the country when communists staged a coup-d'état and killed those who disagreed with them. He escaped to Sweden through a miraculous chain of events and earned a PhD in economic development from the University of Stockholm.

On my trip to Kenya, I saw low-fee, independent schools for the first time. Makonen and I were impressed by how much the schools could do with so little. We saw firsthand that they were financially sustainable. School owners could net $200–$400 per month, a decent livelihood for them. Hardworking school entrepreneurs were in humble towns and villages across the globe, and we had had no idea.

These school owners were "edupreneurs," education entrepreneurs who start schools or institutions. I loved the concept of Christian edupreneurs, but I was skeptical that schools could be financially sustainable by charging just fifty cents or a dollar a day and still repay a loan. How was that possible? But Makonen and I saw it firsthand. Also, Bob Pattillo, another friend who learned about the opportunity of low-fee independent schools, had been a successful real estate developer. He immediately formed the Indian School Finance Corp and started making loans in that country. Bob went on to make thousands of school loans to low-fee independent schools educating millions of children.

Unfortunately, the program of school loans developed more slowly than I would have liked at Opportunity International. The board of directors was not nearly as enthusiastic about making loans to schools as I was.

A NEW ORGANIZATION

I then spent several months seeking the Lord about what He wanted me to do next. I began to feel His clear call to start a new organization, Edify.org, that focused on expanding and improving Christ-centered schools educating children living in poverty in Africa and Latin America. I came to believe this was a great path to profound and long-lasting transformation for millions of children.

Shortly thereafter, I was invited to an event put on by the Halftime Institute, which helps people transition from successful careers to social entrepreneurship and other pursuits to help others. Founded by Bob Buford and Lloyd Reeb, Halftime's managing director at the time was Tiger Dawson. I had just read a Halftime publication featuring one hundred social entrepreneurs affiliated with Halftime. I wondered what I needed to achieve to be listed among those hundred people in a future year. Tiger surprised me by calling me to the front where I was presented with the Bob Buford Halftime Achievement Award given to one person annually.

Invited to the microphone, I then spoke about my personal journey from "success to significance," a phrase coined by Bob Buford and Lloyd Reeb. Tiger paid close attention, and we talked afterward. He loved what I was planning with Christian schools in Africa and Latin America. Sometime later, Tiger expressed an interest in joining me. My response was, "Wow! That would be great!"

When word got out that Tiger might leave Halftime, two dozen other organizations tried to recruit him. But as we talked, he grew more excited about what we might do together. He decided to join me, and we cofounded Edify together.[10]

> *Often when you respond to the Lord's call, the Lord brings great people alongside you!*

My transition to social entrepreneurship was reasonably smooth for several reasons:

1. *I didn't give up a business.* I had sold my business and was free to explore other avenues. Frankly, after two years of only serving on boards after selling the company, I felt restless—that I was not achieving much. This verse convicted me: "From the one who has been entrusted with much, much more will be asked" (Luke 12:48).

2. *There was little downside.* That being said, when I presented the idea of joining a microfinance organization to my YPO peer consulting forum, all seven members advised me against it. Going from business to a nonprofit was totally off their radar screens. Traveling so much, often to poor African countries, made no sense to them. However, my longtime mentor and role model of a Christian entrepreneur, Merrill Oster, encouraged me to go forward. He asked, "What is your downside? If it doesn't work out, you can go back into business. But if you sense the Lord is calling you to Christian microfinance, you should follow that call."

3. *I felt called.* In my heart I felt like this was something God was calling me to do, and my most trusted advisor, the person who knew me best, my wife, Jane, encouraged me to take the leap.

4. *Microfinance organizations are more similar to business than many other nonprofits.* I was aware that not all my experience would transfer to the social sector. I once heard a colorful business school professor, Warren McFarlan, tell a group of experienced businesspeople interested

in serving on nonprofit boards, "You executives think that all of the principles you have learned in the for-profit world transfer to nonprofit operations. But they don't." He continued, in a dramatic voice, while pointing his finger at us. "Only half of your principles apply. And the problem is you don't know which half applies!" This prompted a good laugh from the audience along with numerous heads nodding in affirmation. I took the professor's words to heart. When I planned on instituting changes, I spent more time listening to the senior leadership team at the nonprofit before making those changes than I would have at my for-profit company.

When the decision-making time came on taking the job, I pictured myself at ninety years old sitting in a rocking chair and looking back on my life. I thought, *Would I have greater joy knowing I made more money or helped many people?* I knew the answer was the latter.

Numerous challenges occurred on the social entrepreneurship path, including being misunderstood and even falsely accused of wrong motives by some I served. However, there have been so many more wonderful, fulfilling times.

My friendships with other Christian social entrepreneurs go to profound levels among those who serve God's materially impoverished. I have great joy in knowing the Lord used me to be a part of approximately four million people receiving microfinance loans and approximately three million children living in poverty benefiting from improvements in their Christian education. I would not trade that for having continued in business these last twenty years, even if business had brought great success.

At Edify, we now have a much bigger vision. We hope to reach 100 million children with quality Christian education. As the internet becomes more widely available in developing nations at lower prices, many more parents living on just several dollars a day will be able to afford it. Whereas the majority of the 3 million children in Edify partner schools currently have no textbooks or any other books, with inexpensive digital tablets in the future they can have digital textbooks, reading books, animated videos, free digital curriculum such as Khan Academy, and many other free resources to greatly improve their education and Christ-centered character.

As you decide your future path, consider the late Professor Clayton Christensen's *Harvard Business Review* article titled "How Will You Measure Your Life?" He ended the article by saying:

> I've concluded that the metric by which God will assess my life isn't dollars but the individual people whose lives I've touched. I think that's the way it will work for us all. Don't worry about the level of individual prominence you have achieved; worry about the individuals you have helped become better people. This is my final recommendation: Think about the metric by which your life will be judged, and make a resolution to live every day so that in the end, your life will be judged a success.[11]

Professor Christensen was right regarding how we will judge ourselves. Although Lloyd and I have traveled on different journeys, we both have experienced the profound joys of benefiting many other people—100x more than we would have if we had stayed in regular business careers. Social entrepreneurs focus on benefiting others and helping them become better people. They do this by becoming their own Chief Life Officer, which we describe in the next chapter.

> SOCIAL ENTREPRENEURS FOCUS ON BENEFITING OTHERS.

4

BECOMING A CHIEF LIFE OFFICER

The Pursuit of Intentionality Without Insisting on Control

THE LATE DR. HOWARD HENDRICKS, a renowned Bible scholar, said most of the leaders in the Bible did not finish well.[12] In other words, if you list out all the leaders mentioned in the Bible and study how their lives ended, many, if not most, did not appear to flourish at the end of their lives. Think of Moses, Samson, or Solomon, to name just a few. In more recent terms, Dr. Bobby Clinton's study of 3,500 Christian leaders revealed that only a third finish well.[13] In like manner, social entrepreneurs often fail, not because their organizations aren't effective, but because they don't manage the broader elements of their lives well. Eventually, it catches up with them. What would it look like for you to finish well?

Your work is one important aspect of your life story, but it's not the most important. We want to help you think way ahead and reflect on the bigger picture. How can you *sustain* a life of service, sacrifice, and significance? This is part of your work, being your own Chief Life Officer. This requires taking responsibility for your whole life, which includes shaping and owning the long-term vision and the underlying values and commitments and the pathway to get from where you are to where you desire to be, taking those you love on the journey with you. Endeavoring to live with a high degree of intentionality, without insisting on control. We believe this is the pathway to being the soil that produces 100x.

Again, let's turn to renowned business school professor Clayton Christensen, famed for coining the phrases "disruptive innovation" and the "innovator's dilemma." He speaks of the personal failures of many of the Harvard MBAs in his class:

> Over the years I've watched the fates of my HBS classmates from 1979 unfold; I've seen more and more of them come to reunions unhappy, divorced, and alienated from their children. I can guarantee you that not a single one of them graduated with the deliberate strategy of getting divorced and raising children who would become estranged from them. And yet a shocking number of them implemented that strategy. The reason? They didn't keep the purpose of their lives front and center as they decided how to spend their time, talents, and energy.[14]

We have been helping successful business and social sector leaders for more than twenty years. Lloyd has spent over twenty thousand hours coaching them, and Chris has mentored many. We have watched them do amazing things. Here are some highlights we've witnessed over the years:

- Helping the financially impoverished work their way out of poverty through microfinance.
- Building thousands of houses for families in Latin America.
- Organizing affordable medical clinics in Africa serving people who could not get medical care anywhere else.
- Drilling wells to provide clean water in African and Indian villages.
- Reinventing mental wellness care.
- Helping children in developing nations gain a good education through financially sustainable Christian schools.

- Building the largest inner-city Little League baseball league.
- Bringing many US farmers to Albania with new farming techniques and the good news of Jesus.

While some of these talented leaders are finishing well, others are not. What makes the difference?

KEY CHARACTERISTICS OF A STRONG CHIEF LIFE OFFICER

Having studied this narrow slice of leaders up close over many years, we have learned a few key elements that make it more likely for someone to finish well. The most important one we talked about already:

Getting clear and convinced of your calling, which will give you staying power.

Keep building on a solid foundation. As a founding entrepreneur, your enterprise must rest on a solid foundation. How many people have created remarkable organizations, only to sabotage them later in life by failing to keep their personal and moral life strong? You build a great life from the inside out. If you are going to make a lasting impact over the long haul, your life and worldview must be built on a solid foundation. Then you must regularly get detailed feedback about how the inner elements of your world are doing.

The exercise below was developed by Bob Shank, founder of The Master's Program (themastersprogram.org), to assess your life in three concentric circles: your inside world, your surrounding world, and your outside world. It has helped many people get perspective on their lives. This exercise involves scoring yourself for each of these factors on a scale of 1–10 where 1 means you are not excelling and 10 means you are. Ask your spouse or close friend to score you as well, then have a conversation about why they scored you the way they did (both high and low scores) and what you can learn from their input.[15]

YOUR INSIDE WORLD

Personal Growth: To what extent are you learning and growing?

Health: To the degree you can control it, how healthy are you?

Marriage: If you are married, to what degree is your marriage thriving?

Faith: How connected are you with Jesus, in a living, daily relationship?

YOUR SURROUNDING WORLD

Career: To what degree has your career been successful and God-honoring?

Parenting/Grandparenting: If you are a parent, to what degree are you connected with and leading your children and grandchildren?

Friendships: How are you doing at cultivating deep friendships?

Finances: How effectively have you, and are you, stewarding your finances?

YOUR OUTSIDE WORLD

Community Impact: To what degree are you making a positive impact in your community?

Global Impact: To what degree are you making a positive impact nationally or internationally?

The purpose of this exercise is to allow you to identify areas in your inside world and surrounding world that need to be improved to have a solid foundation on which to build the impact in your outside world.

What are the two or three areas you are most motivated to focus on?

Areas you want to improve:	What will you do?
_____	_____
_____	_____
_____	_____

Engage those closest to you in ongoing accountability in these areas.

Create spiritual rhythms. A spiritual rhythm is a set of habitual activities that you have discovered over time to help you stay connected to God in a deep and meaningful way. John 15:5 says if we stay connected to the Vine, we will produce much fruit. What spiritual rhythms will enable you to stay connected to God?

- Daily time with God. Identify when, where, and how this will happen.
- Regular silent spiritual retreats. Block them off on your calendar each quarter.
- A personal board of directors of wise, godly people. Jot down two or three names. (Read more about this in Chapter 7.)

Prioritize healthy habits. My mentor, Bob Buford, once asked me (Lloyd) to make two lists side-by-side on a sheet of paper. On the left I was to list everything I have that is valuable. I quickly jotted down valuable items like my business, investments, classic cars, etc., with a warm sense of accomplishment. Then he said, "Now on the right side, write down everything you have that is priceless. And then let's talk about how you are protecting those items."

That caught me completely off guard, and I was surprised at how few items are truly priceless. I was tempted to put my business on the priceless list, but it has a value. As we talked about what I was doing to protect those things, I discovered the valuable items were carefully protected and insured, but many of the priceless items were largely unprotected.

Take a minute and try this exercise before reading on.

Valuable	Priceless
_____	_____
_____	_____
_____	_____
_____	_____

It never makes sense to trade what is priceless for what is just valuable. So let's focus on health for a second.

After doing this exercise with many mentees, I noticed some trends. Our health is priceless, yet many people don't get the sleep, exercise, or nutrition they need to thrive, which dramatically affects their impact over time. As your organization grows and deeply helps people, you might be tempted to put your ministry over your health, but that's not a good trade.

Take a quick skim down this checklist of some important elements:

- Do you get enough sleep? Studies show very few people operate at their best with less than eight hours of sleep.
- Do you have a routine of exercise every day?
- Have you decided what your optimal weight is? Pick a weight that you feel is in your *own best interest,* and then weigh yourself regularly. If you creep up, lose a few pounds. Like the saying goes, "You stay fit in the gym, but trim in the kitchen."

- Do you track your data? (annual checkup, your blood work numbers, blood pressure, etc.)
- How do you maintain flexibility/balance?

What commitments are you most motivated to make to protect your health? Your impact as a social entrepreneur will be directly linked to your health and wellness, not only in terms of how long you can work at it, but the energy, creativity, and focus that you bring.

Build a plan for financial freedom versus financial independence. You want to focus on helping people rather than being concerned about money. But if you don't have a financial plan, you will likely end up spending way more emotional energy worried about money over time. God is your provider, and He wants you to enjoy what He gives you. But you are also a steward of what He gives you, which means you are responsible to use the resources God gives you to invest them on His behalf. This takes wisdom and planning. Having a clear financial plan will free your mind to focus on being a good kingdom investor of your time and resources.

Our advice is to:

- Decide on the optimal lifestyle by balancing family needs, comfort, and long-term security, thereby minimizing the stress you feel to produce cash flow.
- Find a trusted financial advisor (kingdomadvisors.com).
- Create a spending plan based on that lifestyle, and then track it monthly.
- Build a long-term financial plan that helps you be generous as well as provide for kids' college and weddings, medical care, retirement, etc.

We have both found great joy in the freedom that comes from having a clear financial plan, setting some limits on what we will spend on ourselves, and the adventure of seeing how God provides abundantly over many years.

Get clear on your family vision and values. One of the things you value most is your family. If your family is not doing well, you might need to change your approach to living out your vocational calling. Your family could be going along just fine, or perhaps it has pockets of conflict or pain. You might be single and part of a broader family, or you might be an empty nester. Regardless of your family makeup, investing in family is a key to thriving in life and finishing well.

> INVESTING IN FAMILY IS A KEY TO THRIVING IN LIFE AND FINISHING WELL.

Building a thriving family requires *leadership* and *intentionality*. Here are four helpful components:

- Infuse the Bible and prayer into daily family routines.
- Create a family vision statement.
- Define your family values.
- Build on each other's strengths.

It's never too early or too late to begin partnering with God and tapping into His wisdom for your family. Because this last key is so important, we want to spend a little more time on it.

FOCUS ON THE FAMILY

Linda and Lloyd have been married for more than forty years, have three children who are married, and have new family members being born into the family every year. Their family gatherings are filled with laughter, tears, honest conversations, uniquely different personalities, things that go as planned, and things that don't—but when those special times are over, and they are alone again, they are filled with overwhelming gratitude. Not gratitude because they somehow "orchestrated" a thriving family but because they have benefited from applying the Bible's wisdom in their family and because God's help has been very real and personal.

Psalm 127:1 says, "Unless the Lord builds the house, the builders labor in vain." Notice this verse does not minimize the role of the builders, but if we try to build a great family without aligning with God and His work, we are missing out! So how can we partner with God in building our family?

Deuteronomy 6:6–7 tells us: "These commandments that I give you today are to be on your hearts. Impress them on your children. Talk about them when you sit at home and when you walk along the road, when you lie down and when you get up." Let's make God's Word central in our homes.

Begin family dinners with heartfelt prayer. Begin each day with a short Bible reading at breakfast. (We recommend a simple YouVersion plan: youversion.com.) One of Chris's friends was the CEO of an international airline. He told Chris that he prayed for an hour every morning. Further, he believed he got more done on the days when he prayed than when he thought he was too busy to pray. Former President George W. Bush, in his book *Decision Points,* said he started every day of his eight years as president the same way he had started every day prior to becoming president: he read his Bible. If these two extremely busy people found time to read the Bible and pray every morning, we can as well.

Lloyd's family has a large chalkboard in the kitchen, and Linda writes a Bible verse of the week at the top. It allows God to prompt her about what her family needs at that moment. These verses quietly sit there as the family cooks, eats, and plays games. One day Lloyd asked his adult daughter what had contributed to their family health. She answered, "The Bible memorization on weekends. Even though we didn't enjoy it at the time, you were hiding God's Word in our hearts." The simple habit of memorizing some Bible verses worked its way into their subconscious and shaped their worldviews.

The Bible says, "The wise woman builds her house" (Prov. 14:1). But most of the time we feel like we lack the wisdom for the challenges in our family. It is critical to spend time with God as husband and wife and pray for your family and for wisdom.

Create a vision statement for your family. Leading your family involves having a vision for your family and values that support your vision. Proverbs 29:18 says, "Where there is no vision, the people perish" (KJV). Where there is no vision the family drifts, and it's not always in the same direction.

Creating a vision statement for your family is as simple as writing down what you really want your family to be like way down the road. (If you are single or divorced, your vision for your family might need to be implemented in a more nuanced way; however, it's still a helpful tool to enable you to shape this important element in life.) It's funny that when we say that someone's building their "dream home," we know exactly what they mean. It's a compilation of all they most value wrapped up into one home. Having a vision for your family is really the ultimate dream home.

> HAVING A VISION FOR YOUR FAMILY IS REALLY THE ULTIMATE DREAM HOME.

Bert Parker is a radiologist, his kids are grown, and he's been in a yearlong roundtable with peers working on what's next in his life. For our last meeting, I asked everyone to bring an artifact of what God had done in and through their family over the year. Bert came with this big object wrapped in brown paper, which he unveiled for the group. It was a framed version of their new family vision. It hangs in their kitchen as an ongoing reminder of what they wish their family to become. Here is what it says:

THE PARKER FAMILY LEGACY

An unbroken chain of followers of Jesus. Each thriving in their spiritual lives. Abundantly living out God's unique design and calling. Joyfully encouraging and supporting one another. Exhibiting grace and generosity. Being salt and light within a broken world.

Think about that vision for a second. Imagine if this vision were true of your family in thirty years!

Instill values for your family. After you have a vision for your family, establish values to undergird the vision. Values give you tracks to run on and motivate how you respond to life decisions. For example, in 2002, we (Lloyd and Linda) gathered our family around a bonfire and asked our children to tell us honestly what they thought was working in our family and what wasn't. Out of that conversation came five values that we agreed on, wrote down, and posted on the fridge: godliness (reflecting God's love and character); love in action; creating memories together; celebrating individual interests; and enthusiasm.

Those simple values have had an unbelievable impact on our family since then. For example, the value of "creating memories together" helped us edit out less important activities so we could focus on making memories. Of course, we didn't execute those five values perfectly—not even close to perfectly—but we discovered that a little bit goes a very long way.

Use your strengths to serve your family. Building a thriving family requires leadership. All of us can take a proactive leadership role in building up our family, regardless of its makeup. So, let's lead from our strengths. First Peter 4:10 says, "Each of you should use whatever gift you have received to serve others." Help your family know each other's strengths, so they can all contribute well. As our families grow, we can remind them that they each have different strengths to contribute, and those strengths are for service—not status.

Your family is unique with unique opportunities and challenges. God put leaders in every family to actively bring their wisdom and creativity to help the family thrive. Lloyd's youngest daughter, Jennie, has the strength of encouragement and adaptability, so she is a wonderful shock absorber in the family. Linda's strength is a researcher and mentor who works at finding resources for each family member when a need arises and arranging travel and creative lodging for family vacations. Their son, Carter, is empathetic and brings real depth to relationships as new family members have married into the family.

THE FOUNDATION, NOT A FRILL

If you take charge of your personal life as Chief Life Officer, and build on a solid foundation of faith rhythms, financial wisdom, thoughtful fitness, and investing in thriving family habits, your social enterprise will have a much greater chance of transforming the lives of many people for many years. This is a key ingredient to making a 100x contribution in this world, as your ministry impact will compound over time.

5

GAINING 100X YIELD

Exponential Impact

YOU HAVE LIKELY discovered your passion and your core contribution and find great joy when you see the real impact in others' lives. You share stories with your family and friends about how your organization makes a difference. But in your heart you might wonder, *If only I could find a way to impact 30x, 60x, or 100x that number of people and in even deeper ways.* From our observations, leaders who make 100x impact do it by using leverage, as described in Chapter 1 and below. Not by just running faster and longer. That is a sure path to burnout. So how can we help you gain more leverage?

Seasoned social entrepreneurs who are in their seventies or eighties who truly contribute seldom are in a rush.

Lloyd saw this in Bob Buford's life and talked with him about it one day. Bob said such individuals have likely answered two essential questions: What is my calling? How will I gain leverage?

It's helpful to think through four areas of leverage for your social enterprise: the platform,

> HOW WILL I GAIN LEVERAGE?

the processes, the people, and the power of the Spirit of God. Before we jump in, why should we plan for leverage or scaling up the work to which we are called? Is bigger always better? What if you're called just to serve a few people? Won't scaling your organization risk making a name for yourself and resulting in pride regarding your contribution? In our view the simple answer is that we seek leverage in a desire to benefit as many people as possible.

What if each of us set our sights on being the soil that produced 100x? Let's dive into four ways we can do that.

PLATFORM

You can design your enterprise as a platform(s) to help you live out your personal mission. Based on your personal mission statement, strengths, and personality, what kind of platform will best multiply your impact? Also, would you see the best results by using several platforms that complement each other?

For example, my primary platform is the Halftime Institute, but I also use the YPO (Young Presidents' Organization) platform, Legatus, Tiger 21, and other similar organizations that convene groups of highly successful business leaders. My role as the founding partner of the Halftime Institute enhances my abilities to reach CEOs through the YPO or Legatus platforms.

Here are five important elements of designing your creative platform:

1. *How much structure?* How much structure do you need to thrive? By structure we mean the processes, people, and systems to support your work. If you have worked in big complex organizations, you may need more structure. Lloyd does best with very little structure, which lends itself to building a movement that is loosely organized.

2. *Desired impact?* In other words, your Great Commandment or Great Commission impact. Imagine if you could design an organization that produced the impact that you most desire. Do you feel called to more of a "Great Commission type" impact (making disciples) or

"Great Commandment type" impact (loving your neighbor)? Jesus told us to do both, but you might feel called to one more than the other.

3. *Cause or contribution focus?* Is your calling specific to a cause/group of people, or are you called to a specific kind of contribution that could easily apply to many causes or people groups? Chris focuses on a cause of microfinance in helping the poor. While Lloyd cares about many compassionate causes, he remains focused on his contribution and is cause-neutral.

4. *Place or portfolio?* Do you operate best with multiple things going on in multiple organizations, or if you focus on one organization at a time? Many leaders do their best when they are all in, totally focused on one organization and one team. They love showing up every day and making the "20 Mile March," as coined by Jim Collins.[16] Others do their best work by getting something going, building momentum, and then looking around at other opportunities that fit their calling and bringing that same intensity to the next project. But the risk with a portfolio approach is not being fully present when you are with one group or working on one project. While Lloyd has stayed focused on the Halftime movement for over twenty years, he has always worked on launching the movement in new countries and into new market niches with new team members.

Chris, by contrast, has been a serial entrepreneur, typically growing an organization for seven years, and then handing it off. Each experience has better equipped him for the next entrepreneurial role.

5. *Your roles?* Almost every platform provides opportunities for directly serving people, managing the organization, or strategizing roles such as board roles, mentor roles, silent partner roles, ambassador roles, etc. How do you want to allocate your time between these three categories: serving, managing, and strategizing? Because Lloyd is a thought leader entrepreneur and not an organizational leader, he takes no management roles. Instead, most of his time is in direct service, with a third of his time allocated to the global movement of Halftime.

The big idea we want you to take away from this discussion of platform is that you can think through and design your platform intentionally so it aligns well with your strengths and your desires—making it more sustainable.

PROCESSES

Second, you can leverage processes. What processes can you develop or onboard that will extend your impact far beyond your effort and time? When your process is still working and you are not, this is leverage.

Chris gains leverage through the processes he has developed and refined at Edify as the organization provides loans and training to 12,000 Christian schools educating 3.2 million children in developing countries. Edify leverages existing Christian schools, Christian microfinance institutions, school associations, and technology to reach 20–30 percent more children every year. Lloyd gains leverage through the processes defined in books, the curriculum, and the coaching training that ultimately serves thousands of people around the world—often many time zones away while he is sleeping. These processes comprise all they have learned, all the tools someone needs in one place. Every day Lloyd can simply point a person to the best tool for them, and they can begin moving forward on their own.

Here are a couple of other examples: Allister Hannah was the managing partner of McKinsey & Company's consulting office in Manhattan when he felt called to launch a social enterprise to help seekers explore Christianity. He gained immense leverage by finding a proven process in the Alpha program from the UK. Also, Ken Blanchard, the business author and consultant, decided servant leadership was a missing piece in corporate America and believed Jesus was the greatest leader of all time who modeled servant leadership. He gained 100x impact by creating a process and curriculum that is used all over the world called *Lead like Jesus*. We personally saw it working powerfully in India long after Ken's last trip there.

Make a list of the processes for your organization that could be further refined and packaged. This will allow you to leverage your experience and expertise, making them consistently repeatable by many others. What are one or two key processes you could develop?

> WHAT ARE ONE OR TWO KEY PROCESSES YOU COULD DEVELOP?

YOUR PEOPLE

The third element of creating leverage is people. Whom do you need around you, and in what roles do you need them to gain 100x impact from each unit of effort or each dollar you invest?

A great example of this was Bill Bright, the founder of CRU (Campus Crusade for Christ), who hired a young MBA every few years to travel with him and handle any follow-up commitments. This not only extended his reach as his energy lessened in his seventies, but he also mentored more than twenty young men who have now become world-class leaders.

Lloyd was recently in Hong Kong and Taiwan. In those countries, David Wong, who was the deputy CEO of the Bank of China, leads Halftime. After just a few years in leadership, David has a team of very talented Halftime alumni who are table leaders and coaches. David leverages not only the Halftime platform, brand, and process but also several very talented leaders to be able to serve dozens of Halftimers. He only dedicates about a third of his time to Halftime, which enables him to be on four corporate boards and have plenty of time to visit his kids around the world.

Make a list of the kind of roles you need around you to scale your organization, perhaps labeled by their unique abilities rather than just job titles. You might not be able to fill all those slots, but having them in mind will enable you to spot them when they cross your path.

THE POWER OF THE SPIRIT OF GOD

The fourth area of leverage is the power of the Spirit of God. What do you need to do to systematically listen more clearly to the Spirit of God? If you look throughout history, God used platforms, processes, and people. And sometimes He worked without any of those.

Bill Bright's ministry, which we referenced earlier, has tens of thousands of people bringing the message of Jesus all around the world, and Bill is in heaven now. But when you study Bill's life, you find that his secret sauce was his ability to quietly listen to the promptings of God and then follow God's leading.

Here are a few common ingredients in people's lives who are good at leveraging the power of the Spirit of God:

- They try to eliminate hurry from their lives.
- They have time each morning to be quiet and pray, listen to God, and meditate on His Word.
- They take time regularly to get away for a silent spiritual retreat.
- They fast when they especially need to hear from God.
- They surround themselves with wise counselors (e.g., a personal board of directors).

The verses in Acts 13:1–3 are striking:

> Among the prophets and teachers of the church at Antioch of Syria were Barnabas, Simeon (called "the black man"), Lucius (from Cyrene), Manaen (the childhood companion of King Herod Antipas), and Saul. One day as these men were worshiping the Lord and fasting, the Holy Spirit said, "Appoint Barnabas and Saul for the special work to which I have called them." So after more fasting and prayer, the men laid their hands on them and sent them on their way. (NLT)

As we see, Barnabas and Saul had a diverse set of friends around them, relied on them for perspective, and together gave careful thought and prayer to their strategy—which gave them confidence as they set off on an adventure together. Make a list of the people you wish to play this role.

YOUR LEVERAGE

Take a minute now and summarize your thinking around these four areas of leverage.

- What would your best *platform* look like?
- What *processes* are still needed or need to be improved to provide the most leverage?
- What *people* do you need to add or remove to gain the most leverage?
- How can you better listen to and align with the *power of the Spirit of God*?

With clarity about the kind of organization you are building, and your own unique strengths, calling, and long-term desires, we will now turn our attention to your team. How will you build a world-class team with the resources you have?

PART 2

THE SOCIAL ENTREPRENEUR'S TEAM

6

BUILDING A WORLD-CLASS TEAM ON STARTUP FUNDING

IMAGINE THE FUTURE joy when you are surrounded by talented leaders who love the vision for your organization, have deep abiding ownership of the mission, can solve their own problems while still aligning with the values and strategy set by the management team, grow the impact exponentially, and love working together. Building a world-class team like that for your social enterprise has two major components: hiring and grooming paid staff, and then thinking broader than staff to building a world-class team of non-staff that you simply could not afford to hire.

Think about these questions before we get started:

- What are the best practices for hiring and managing great staff?
- What would make your team world-class?
- Could your team be much broader than just paid staff?
- How can you afford a world-class team now?

You will find the answers to these questions below.

BEST PRACTICES FOR HIRING AND MANAGING A GREAT TEAM

A highly successful entrepreneur friend of mine says,

> *"Hiring is the most important decision a CEO/ED makes."*

Here are our best practices in simple point form so you can reference them over and over as a checklist.

SELECTING STAFF

Hire and retain only "A-players." A-players hire A-players, and B-players hire C-players. If you wish to avoid ending up with an organization riddled with C-players, you need to hire and retain only A-players. A-players are not only very good at what you need them to do, but they also have a great attitude, are enthusiastic/passionate about the work your organization does, and are a good culture fit with your organization. If they do not have all four, they are not an A-player.

Don't retain a B-player or C-player longer than ninety days. We recommend that you have at least a ninety-day probation period for everyone hired. Ask yourself or the new hire's manager on day eighty why the person is an A-player. If a good case cannot be made that the person is an A-player, do them and yourself a favor by letting them go before the probation period ends. Rarely do people turn around and become better performers. If there is some evidence but not clear evidence the new hire is an A-player, then extend the probationary period another ninety days. This puts the new hire on notice that they may possibly still be a fit, but they must prove it by good performance. Although this may sound harsh, you are serving disadvantaged people who deserve to have the best performers you can hire. In addition, as a good steward, you will wish to pay only those staff who share your values, are passionate about serving, and are doing an excellent job.

To assess their competency before hiring them, ask yourself, *Does this person's track record strongly indicate that they have the skills and drive to be successful given the requirements of the job I wish to fill?* Make a list of the reasons the person will do a good job for you. Then make a list of your concerns of why they might not be able to do a good job. This analysis will illuminate and inform your decision about extending an offer letter.

The candidate must be passionate about your work. How will you know if they are truly in love with what you do? Ask questions that will reveal if the person has made significant efforts to serve people similar to those you serve. Listen carefully to their tone when discussing your work. Is there true enthusiasm and passion in their voice and body language?

As soon as anyone on your team wishes to extend an offer letter to a candidate, before the offer letter is sent, then you, as the CEO/ED, should interview that candidate. This is true even if the candidate is an entry-level person and you have fifty or more employees already. In this case, you and the HR director might spend only ten minutes with the candidate.

> But you must believe the candidate is an A-player before the offer letter goes out.

This does not mean you will interview every applicant, but you will interview people your managers have decided should be hired, even if a person's job is entry level or otherwise low-paid. Naturally, you need to personally interview fully every candidate for a senior executive position who makes it through the initial screening process. In the early stages of your enterprise when you have less than fifty employees, you will do well to fully interview every applicant who makes it through your initial screens when only three candidates remain. Be sure to have a streamlined system that responds rapidly to applicants, as excellent candidates may get job offers quickly from other employers.

Managers in your organization will be much more selective if they know the CEO/ED will interview the person before they are hired. They will also raise their standards as you explain to them why you have turned down some of the people they wanted to hire. When I (Chris) started doing this at my organization, I rejected 30 percent of the candidates that managers wished to hire. I explained to them the shortcomings I identified. Within six months, I was only rejecting 10 percent of the candidates because the managers had raised their standards.

MOST COMMON MISTAKES IN HIRING AND FIRING

"We need somebody right away." Avoid hiring someone who may not be qualified just because of an urgency to fill a position. Remember how uncomfortable it was to fire the last person who did not work out.

Hiring someone based on a single issue rather than carefully considering numerous attributes and shortcomings of the person. For example, an extroverted manager might be inclined to hire an extroverted assistant because of their personality even though the manager needs someone who is very detail oriented.

Not interviewing a candidate enough times on enough different days. By interviewing the candidate on two or more days, inconsistencies in their story may become apparent if they are not being fully transparent about their background or what they are telling you.

Not having enough members of your team interview the candidate. Appoint a team member to be "the challenger." This person makes a case against hiring the candidate.

Not documenting poor performance in writing and then sharing the documentation of poor performance with the staff member. Sometimes managers finally get up enough courage to let a person go, only to have HR or their labor lawyer say sufficient documentation is absent regarding coaching and warnings given to the poor performer.

Not giving new hires sufficient training to be successful in their jobs. If they do not have significant prior experience in a similar role, make sure adequate coaching to do the job well is provided.

Not having a well-conceived and well-implemented onboarding process for new hires. Determine the information needed for new hires to understand the big picture and the important contribution their job makes. Convey this in an inspirational manner. Share the culture of your organization. Make efforts to cordially introduce new hires to new coworkers.

Not having each person on your team who interviews a candidate fill out a weighting and rating sheet on the candidate based on the criteria you have determined for the job. (For a sample rating sheet, please refer to the endnotes.)[17] After each interviewer has filled out the form, all should meet as soon as possible and make a recommendation to the CEO/ED to do the final interview with the person or let the candidate know they will not receive an offer.

Not having an "interview review" form. This is a half-page form filled out by the candidate about to receive a job offer. It asks, "Have you been promised anything other than your starting salary, job location, and your job title? If so, please describe that promise in writing below." This simple form will avoid employees claiming later that you made promises that you never did. You will be amazed at how many employees sincerely think promises were made to them that actually never were. This form has saved Chris much time, legal fees, and heartache with people who claim promises were made to them. We show them the form they signed and where they said no promises were made. It is incumbent upon HR to review all these forms before an offer letter goes out to make sure any promises the candidate indicated are correct. (Consult the endnotes for a sample interview review template.)[18]

Not making sure the board understands that you, as CEO/ED, make all hire/fire decisions regarding staff. If your board meddles in hiring and firing, this will lead to excessive politics, significantly increased headaches for you, and suboptimal recruiting, retention, and performance.

If the board does not allow the CEO/ED to make hire/fire decisions, how can the board hold the CEO/ED accountable for the performance of the organization if they are not empowered to select the team? A lack of hire/fire authority means you are not truly the CEO/ED.

Hiring job hoppers. You will have applicants who, in their last several positions, have not stayed with any organization for two or more years. It will likely be a net loss to your organization if someone stays two years or less. You will have invested time and money in this person and likely have not received a good return. Job hoppers, when asked if they will stay three years or more with your organization, almost always say they will stay because they are looking for an organization at which they can work long term. However, their actions speak louder than their words. They always have lots of reasons why they left the other jobs. My favorite was a man who had stayed less than a year in each of his last three jobs. He said he had experienced bad management in each case. I told him that I could predict his opinion of our organization in several months—bad management. I politely explained we would not give him the opportunity to reach that conclusion. Do not even interview job hoppers, which unfortunately is quite common among people in their twenties and thirties.

Not carefully checking statements on an applicant's résumé. A forensic résumé investigator once said on a panel I heard that 73 percent of all résumés contain material misstatements. Ask the university if the degree the candidate claims was actually conferred. Ask if any honors claimed were actually given. You will be surprised how often the answer is no. If an applicant makes false statements on their résumé, you cannot expect them to act with integrity in your organization. Also, be sure to check references. As CEO/ED, you should check some of these references personally on every middle manager or higher. Of course, candidates provide references likely to say good things about them. Ask the references for someone who might be able to tell you of problems with the candidate.

Not carefully listening for inconsistencies in what candidates say during the interview process as compared to the résumé. Be conscious of their body language when asked to explain accomplishments they have highlighted on their résumé. Candidates who fabricate a qualification or accomplishment will often inadvertently give hints to that effect. Watch how candidates treat your receptionist and assistants in your organization. Listen to how they speak about past employers. Are they kind or condescending? Did they use a four-letter word during the interview process or say something else inappropriate? Dismissing his own concern about such an occurrence, Chris once hired a fundraiser who did this. Within six weeks, Chris terminated this fundraiser because the National Christian Foundation informed Chris that the fundraiser told a prospective donor that the Foundation referred the fundraiser to contact the prospective donor. National Christian Foundation does not make such referrals.

Not conducting criminal background checks and requiring drug testing before hiring an applicant. My labor lawyer once said 50 percent of his clients required such testing. He went on to say that applicants who had criminal records or were doing drugs ended up being employed by the 50 percent of his clients not doing such checking and testing. It is easy to assume a nice applicant with whom you are speaking is not involved in such activities. However, this is not always the case. We have been shocked to learn of the serious crimes of which some applicants have been convicted.

With this in mind, we hasten to add that a felony conviction does not necessarily eliminate a person from consideration. A woman once worked at Chris's company as an independent contractor doing field research. She did a very good job, and her supervisor wanted to hire her. The woman was reluctant to apply for the job. Finally, after being asked several times to apply for the job, she revealed that she had been convicted of selling drugs when she was twenty years old and spent time in prison. She was now thirty-seven years old with no run-ins with the law since. Chris consulted HR and a few other senior executives. The woman would not work in accounting or HR or IT or other areas where serious harm could be done. The offer was made to her, which she accepted. Shortly thereafter at the company Christmas party, the woman came to Chris and thanked him and started to cry. Being accepted at the company as a full-fledged employee with benefits was the first time she had felt like a whole person since her criminal conviction. Leave room for redemption; Jesus does this for us.

> LEAVE ROOM FOR REDEMPTION; JESUS DOES THIS FOR US.

Not having good reason to believe a candidate can be successful in the job before making a job offer. It is disruptive for your organization and the candidate's life if you hire them for a position that does not fit their skills. Three of the four reasons that someone is let go are the fault of the organization: the person did not have the skills, was not given the proper training and encouragement, or was not given clear directions needed to do the job well. Employees are at fault when they received the aforementioned but did not conduct themselves in a manner to do the job well.

Not having a board member, mentor, or other advisor with greater expertise than you participate in an important interview. When Chris hired senior executives, he often had his mentor interview them. For forty years the mentor had owned three companies, each with its own president. The mentor had hired dozens of senior executives. This experience had taught him to identify candidates with the highest probability of succeeding.

PAYING FOR TOP TALENT

Hire people who are top-decile performers and pay them accordingly. Often, if you can offer a compensation package 30 percent more than an average performer would receive, you can attract someone who will be two or three times as productive as the average performer. You

> HIRE PEOPLE WHO ARE TOP-DECILE PERFORMERS.

might offer a compensation package slightly above average, with a bonus formula based on strong achievement.

Do not get hung up on paying high performers more than the CEO/ED. Major gift fundraisers raising $2–$4+ million should often be paid more than the CEO/ED. Chris had several such fundraisers and paid them more than anyone else in the organization. They produced several times more value than fundraisers bringing in $500,000 per year.

Rather than raising salaries every year, you may wish to leave salaries the same except for an inflation increase and pay bonuses based on performance each year. This will give you a lot of flexibility if there is a downturn in the economy or if revenues decline in one year. Reducing someone's bonus is much easier than reducing their salary.

PERFORMANCE MANAGEMENT AND GOSPEL-CENTERED FIRING

You do a person a service by compassionately letting them go when they are performing inadequately. It is not "unChristian" to let a low performer go after you have given them a chance to improve. Keeping them will lower the efficiency of your high performers who depend on the low performer. You do a disservice to those your organization serves, as they will receive better services when you replace the low performer with a high performer.

Provide people who are performing insufficiently with regular feedback to this effect. When you must let a person go, get some coaching from an employment lawyer or an experienced HR person. Generally, you want to make only two or three points when the person asks why they are being let go. Stick to those two or three points, even if it means repeating them several times. Avoid bringing out numerous other points that may lead to arguments or turmoil. Pray before letting a person go, and pray for them afterward that they find another organization where their gifts will be a better fit. Give them reasonable severance pay in exchange for a liability release. Do not assume that the release is unnecessary. Too often employers pay severance, thinking,

This employee will never cause trouble, only to be served with a lawsuit a few weeks later.

If you are disciplined in your recruiting process, and place much importance on it, you are highly likely to end up with a great team. This results in tremendous joy as well as being more beneficial to those you seek to serve.

A benefit in leading a cause-oriented organization is that you can acquire talent that you simply cannot afford. Many talented leaders have a desire to make an impact with their life through leveraging their experience, expertise, and network. But many social enterprise leaders are limited in their thinking by ordinary job descriptions and thinking only in terms of either paid staff, board members, or low-level volunteers. That limited perspective might rob you of the ability to gain true partners in your work who do not need to be paid but who would gladly join your team in creative non-staff functions for free.

BUILDING A BROADER TEAM THAN JUST PAID STAFF

For most fast-growing social enterprises, the need for seasoned leadership outstrips the ability to pay for it. The mistake many social enterprises make is hiring the talent they can *afford* rather than the talent they *need*, hoping to turn these individuals into strong leaders. This not only means you lack the talent early when it is so critical but it also fills your ranks with underdeveloped leaders. This scenario can discourage seasoned leaders from joining the team when you can afford them. Often, social entrepreneurs benefit from thinking more creatively about how the most talented leaders can play a role on their team.

> THE MISTAKE MANY SOCIAL ENTERPRISES MAKE IS HIRING THE TALENT THEY CAN *AFFORD* RATHER THAN THE TALENT THEY *NEED*.

If you come from a corporate background or a highly structured nonprofit, you might be tempted to think of your team as the paid staff, with a specific job description, and the board as overseers representing stakeholders. This is a limited perspective. You must define your team more broadly.

A broader view of your team allows you to find the talent you need before you can afford them. Here are some categories to help you begin jotting down your ideas:

- Who are the thought leaders in your movement/space?
- Who in your network has specific expertise and gains joy by sharing their expertise with emerging entrepreneurs?
- What influencers have relational capital and can open doors that you find difficult? For example, recently a rapidly growing nonprofit social enterprise asked Chris for advice on a 50-50 philanthropy/debt model to double the number of houses they were building for people living in poverty. Specifically, they were considering a loan guarantee fund. A dozen years ago, I had done a $10 million loan guarantee fund and was able to attract a prominent law firm to do the legal work *pro bono*. I immediately emailed the loan guarantee private placement memorandum to my friend, explaining that the law firm had put $200,000 of work into the document. This probably will save his social enterprise several months of work and significant expense.
- Who has excess capacity inside their for-profit enterprise and would love to see it used for a social cause? This could be free office space, free legal, accounting, or other professional assistance, equipment no longer needed, etc. For example, when Edify was starting up, a company gave us free office space for four years. I told the company CEO that I prayed for his company to grow, but not so much that they needed to take back our free office space.
- Who can add depth and credibility to your service delivery and does not need to be paid for their valuable time?

- How could those you have already served also serve those you want to serve? Some microfinance organizations encourage their successful clients to hire unemployed people and mentor others receiving their first microfinance loans.

Let me (Lloyd) illustrate this point with stories from my own experience.

Thought Leaders. Very often people who have invested their lives in becoming a thought leader in a particular discipline look for platforms to give back, where that expertise can make a large difference. Joe Miraglia was the head of HR for Motorola back when they had 110,000 employees. He was a thought leader in the corporate leadership training space, having built Motorola University into a flagship model.

When Bob Buford and Lloyd launched the Halftime Institute, they shared with Joe a vision to help some of the most talented business leaders leverage their talent and resources in their second half of life for good, rather than squandering their potential in retirement. Joe was thrilled to help shape the DNA of this global movement.

Who are the most prominent thought leaders in your space? How can you invite them onto your team with specific requests?

Experts. Some leaders have narrow expertise and have a hard time finding ways to use it to help cause-based organizations. Tom McGehee is an expert in adult collaborative learning. He built Ernst & Young's collaborative learning center, where the slogan was "Months of work in days." He was not aware that those exact skills would exponentially advance our work at Halftime helping executives reinvent themselves in midlife. When Bob and Lloyd cast the vision and connected the dots for him, he was all in. His experience opened the gateway for him to help many other social enterprises, and it has been some of the most rewarding work in his life. Make a list of the kinds of expertise you will require as you grow the organization, and then begin networking to see who might have that expertise and would gladly offer it for free if you shared with them the vision for the impact they could make.

Partners. Chances are you will need people who share your vision and can take on new growth opportunities or expansion ideas and become self-directed yet coordinated with your work. A partner is different from staff in that they own the results of your work together just like you do, and they take the initiative to arrange for the resources they need to succeed. Tomas Brunegård came to the Halftime Institute as he approached fifty, wondering, *What's next?* He was the CEO of the largest newspaper chain in Sweden and a well-known executive across Europe. We helped him gain clarity for his life, and through that process he began to see how the Halftime Institute might be the perfect platform for his own work after leaving corporate life. Today he is a partner leading the Halftime Institute in Europe. He took our learning and processes, built his own team, found his own sources of funding, built the brand to create momentum, wrote a book in Swedish, and has served many Halftimers whom we would not have had the capacity to serve.

Influencers. You will encounter people who love what you are doing and have a large following in their city, industry, or network, but don't have the time or interest to roll up their sleeves and grow the organization. They could still join you as an influencer if you provide them with the vision, messaging, communication tools, secretarial assistance, stories they need to get your message to their following with credibility, and a clear call to action.

Kemmons Wilson's family created the Holiday Inn company and has invested deeply in their hometown of Memphis, Tennessee. He was a big fan of business leaders giving back in creative ways and felt Halftime provided the necessary structure and process to help them sort that out. As we launched the Halftime movement in Tennessee, Kemmons got the word out and used his hotels to convene his contacts. We provided the team and process, and he lent his influence, which leveraged his time well. I can still see Kemmons smiling from the back of a room filled with 150 fellow business leaders in Memphis as they explored how they could be part of making Memphis better.

Team Members with Excess Capacity. Are there fans of your organization who are busy with their own careers but have resources or excess capacity that they would gladly provide to you, but it has never crossed their mind? Griff Jones loves sports and helping young athletes become all they can be. His mission is to help a few of the best ministries that help young athletes, but he is very busy running his companies. At one time, he had excess office space in his building, so he offered Fellowship of Christian Athletes the office space for free, and he currently invests a few hours each Monday as a "silent partner"—a safe and confidential sounding board for their regional leaders.

Credibility Partners. Pete Chambers was born into a wealthy family, and then he built on that through his own independent success as an entrepreneur. He sold his company, and today he leads the family office. Together Pete and Lloyd launched a new initiative called the 100x Forum for very successful, affluent men who want their lives to have 100x impact with their time and money. While Lloyd has the expertise and experience to guide these men, Pete is an essential partner in leading the 100x Forum because he brings peer credibility.

While Lloyd has been successful and has had financial freedom for many years, he doesn't have the wealth that 100x Forum members do, so Pete relates to them at a very personal level. Lloyd brings the expertise on midlife renewal, and Pete helps them with the real issues of family relations around wealth, team structure in their family offices, and raising kids who are healthy and wealthy but also wise.

Peers Helping Peers. How could your friends and peers be an adjunct part of your team, perhaps just periodically or a few hours a week? Lloyd's friend Joel Hackney is a serial CEO, currently leading nThrive, which has approximately seven thousand employees around the world. He has used the company as a platform to bless the employees' lives physically, emotionally, and even spiritually. When Lloyd coaches Halftime clients who desire to use their company as a platform for compassion and the gospel, Lloyd introduces them to Joel, who is able to share ideas and best practices for building a company that cares. In this way

Joel is part of Lloyd's team and brings expertise none of the Halftime staff members have . . . and it's free.

As you can see, each of these people brought world-class talent to the team. Talent that the social enterprise could not afford gladly joined the team for free! You will need a broader team than simply paid staff, board members, and donors, but it's up to you as the leader to find them.

> TALENT THAT THE SOCIAL ENTERPRISE COULD NOT AFFORD GLADLY JOINED THE TEAM FOR FREE!

CREATE A CULTURE THAT ATTRACTS TALENTED LEADERS

Take some time to reflect on what would draw the most talented leaders into your organization. What could you do that would interrupt their busy lives, capture their hearts with your vision, help them see where they could easily make a leveraged impact through you and your organization, and feel so comfortable and welcome that they offer to help you? Here are three important elements, but they will require taking some time and getting them right:

Perfect your elevator speech and test it with different audiences. Write out your vision for your organization, including the human need, the reason a social enterprise is the right solution versus a traditional nonprofit or for-profit model, what you envision the organization becoming over time, and a story or two about the impact it makes on people's lives. Share it with some close friends, get their input, and improve it. Then share it in a public setting and see how the audience reacts. Was it coming from your head or your heart? Did any of it feel awkward? Do the words flow out smoothly or feel contrived? Could you tell in their eyes that you touched their hearts? Was it too long or too short? Did it provide a clear next step for them? Write out an improved version and practice it in front of the mirror. Memorize it.

Define opportunities, not needs. Based on your strategy, and the team you have already, what are some of the most important roles people could play to help catapult the progress? Define those opportunities and how they address the need. State the skills required as well as the likely results. Talented leaders are attracted to opportunities, not needs. Paint a picture for them of the joy and blessing it would be for them to help your team change the world.

Let your fruit grow on other people's trees. It's amazing how much you can accomplish if you don't need to take the credit for the accomplishment. Many of the leaders I (Lloyd) described above were looking for a platform where they could make an impact. If you are okay with them owning the results, then they will soon realize you helped them with a platform, brand, process, team, etc., so they can contribute. This turns the recruitment process upside down. I often remind our teams both here and around the world that this is their ministry, and I serve with the desire to be a wind at their back and celebrate how God works through them to advance His kingdom.

If you keep these elements in mind, over time you will create a culture that attracts great leaders.

Hiring only the best people, firing people who don't contribute in a grace-filled way, and building a team of experts, partners, and influencers much broader than just your paid staff are all part of creating a winning culture for your organization. You will be well on your way to producing 100x impact.

7

BUILDING A HIGH-PERFORMANCE BOARD

APPOINTING THE RIGHT people to your board of directors will have a major impact on achieving your vision. Appointing one or more wrong people can devastate your organization. Appointing the right board members is every bit as important as hiring the right executives. A great board member will help move your organization forward significantly and open doors to valuable opportunities and major donors. An ineffective or ill-matched board member can do serious harm and cause such frustration that a CEO/ED may feel the need to leave the organization if the chairman does not act to terminate the misguided board member.

I (Chris) underwent a personal experience of board member troubles. I was CEO of an international microfinance organization, which had grown from $8 million in private funds raised to $51 million during my first six years. The board elected a new chair and vice chair every two years. Having had excellent relationships with the three chairs and vice chairs, I was astonished that everything went south so quickly with the new chair and vice chair. I went from thinking I had the best job in the world to thinking I had the worst job. I resigned after three months of their leadership. The organization then had six CEOs over the next seven years. Its revenues ten years later were about half of the level during my last full year.

Seek to have at least one or two board members in addition to you shortly after startup. Some states may require you to have at least one other board member when incorporating a nonprofit or for-profit. Your first board member besides you should have significant board governance experience! Ideally this person will serve as your board chair unless you have been on numerous boards of directors. Choosing the right chairperson is critical. A good chair will ensure that each new board member added has the skills, time, and enthusiasm to help scale your organization.

Some organizations seek to have a fundraising board, a prestige board, a wealthy donor board, or a high-profile board, all of which may not challenge management's thinking, or worse, sidetrack you. We are believers in appointing board members who can best govern the organization. This means not placing emphasis on board members who can give a lot of money, who are celebrities, or who add diversity for diversity's sake if they do not have needed skills. You'll do best by assembling a board that will challenge your thinking appropriately, bring skills directly relevant to achieving your mission, seek the Lord when advising you, support best governance practices, and spend the time needed to be good directors.

Appointing diverse board members who can make valuable contributions is recommended. For example, thoughtful people from the communities you serve can provide important insights not known to other board members. Thus, we recommend appointing one or two board members from the communities you serve. At a minimum, have such people on your advisory council/board and invite them to speak at board meetings when discussing the communities. If they lack board experience, seek one of your highly experienced trustees to be a resource to assist the board/council member(s) from the communities you serve learn best governance practices.

Having a longtime board member be a resource for every newly appointed director regardless of depth of board experience is a good idea. That resource can help the new director get up to speed more rapidly on the details and nuances of your organization. At Edify we ask a longtime board member to be the "guide" for a newly elected board member. The guide can clarify the structure of Edify and explain jargon and acronyms typically used during board meetings as well as the culture of the board. They can also answer any questions that may come up during the first couple of years of the service of the board member. This guidance helps the new board member understand more and be productive sooner. (Consult the endnotes for a sample of a new board member onboarding process.)[19]

APPOINTING NEW BOARD MEMBERS

Given that each board appointment will either move your mission forward or backward, carefully consider each appointment. When considering director candidates, get advice from people who have served on many boards of directors. Seek a reference from someone who has served on the board with the trustee candidate. I was once asked to be such a reference and felt obligated to report that the trustee candidate was intelligent, personable, and had impressive experience, but had caused harm to the organization on whose board we had served together.

Also, make sure you only appoint board members who are passionate about your primary mission! If they are not passionate, they may sometimes be at odds with you, and then promote initiatives that will take you off mission. If your mission includes helping people economically and sharing Jesus with them, be sure every board candidate is enthusiastic about both aspects of the mission. Do not consider a board candidate, regardless of how good their qualifications are, if they are not truly committed to your total mission. At Edify, if the world's foremost expert on education in developing nations wanted to join our board but was not enthusiastic about sharing Jesus, we would not consider that person.

Have a good "board skill map" that makes it easy to see gaps in the skills that the board seeks. Focus on new board members who bring skills that are not sufficiently represented on the board. (Consult the endnotes for a sample of a board skill map.)[20]

Ask yourself, *Why will this board candidate make a great director? What in the person's background indicates that they will help my organization make better decisions and avoid bad ones? How will they move the needle regarding achieving our mission?* Along with your executives and some or all board members, pray and ask God to confirm if this is the right person. Choosing the right board members and avoiding the wrong ones can make all the difference in your success or failure.

> HOW WILL THEY MOVE THE NEEDLE REGARDING ACHIEVING OUR MISSION?

FOUNDER'S INTENT

Articulate the founder's intent in writing and show this to board candidates. If they are passionate about the founder's intent and vision, you can take the next step and consider their skills. If they are not passionate, do not consider them further. Also, reading the founder's intent document at least once per year at board meetings is a good idea. Some boards read it at the start of every board meeting as an extra step to staying true to mission.

FOURTEEN PRIMARY RESPONSIBILITIES OF A BOARD OF DIRECTORS

Current and prospective board members perform the following key responsibilities well:

1. Guard the mission by ensuring that the organization stays true to its mission, sounding the alarm when there is risk of mission drift, and adjusting policies to stay true to the mission.
2. Ensure that an excellent CEO/ED, who has a strong mission-focused strategy and executes that strategy well, is always in place.

3. Evaluate the CEO/ED annually and provide coaching when appropriate.
4. Have a succession plan for the CEO/ED and update it every two years. (Consult the endnotes for a sample succession plan.)[21]
5. Make good policy decisions and leave day-to-day operations to management.
6. Approve or disapprove significant monetary decisions such as buying a building, signing a long-term lease, acquiring or disposing of significant assets, and partnering in a big way with other organizations.
7. Approve the strategy and any significant additions or changes.
8. Approve the budget.
9. Approve CEO/ED compensation as well as that of other highly compensated executives. (See a comparative compensation survey at thesocialentrepreneur.org/tools.)
10. Challenge management's thinking in a way that encourages them to be better executives.
11. Ensure that management is circumspect of risks and does good enterprise risk management analysis and assessment, which is updated every year. (See Chapter 14 on risk management.)
12. Elect new directors who will guard the mission as well as move the mission forward.
13. Invest the time needed to do an excellent job as a board member.
14. Ensure that appropriate policies are in place and that the board and management follow those policies well.

Having board members who adhere to the above responsibilities will greatly increase the probability that your organization successfully achieves its mission.

FIVE ADDITIONAL RESPONSIBILITIES OF A CHRISTIAN SOCIAL ENTERPRISE BOARD

1. Ensure that the CEO/ED lives a healthy lifestyle regarding faith, family, and work. Are they growing in their faith in Christ and leading staff to grow, not spending too many hours working or traveling away from family?
2. Pray for the organization.
3. Be spiritually discerning and pray when making important decisions, rather than just relying on street smarts and common business practices.
4. Ensure that the mission to involve Jesus is not diluted through donors or other pressures.
5. Live godly lives.

A social enterprise board adhering to the five principles above will take a monumental step toward finishing well.

BOARDS CAN STRESS YOU

I have a friend who is one of the best CEOs I've ever seen among nonprofits or for-profits. Although he has an excellent board, he says that he and other ministry leaders have a lot of anxiety over working with boards. I also have experienced this as CEO. One way to avoid this is to elect the right chairperson. If the chair is well-versed in best governance practices, they can reduce the CEO/ED's stress by intervening when a director is not staying on the policy level but crossing the line into management's purview. A good chair can also resolve issues privately outside of board meetings when appropriate as well as conflicts board members have with the CEO/ED. A good chair is vital for you to be able to focus on your mission rather than board politics.

You, as CEO/ED, run the operations and day-to-day activities. Individual board members can ask you questions about operations, but in no way is it their purview to give instructions to you or your staff.

You report to the entire board, not to any one director, not even the chairman. However, the chairman is the point person for informing you of policies that the board wishes you to implement as well as concerns that directors may have about your performance.

I served on a board where the founder has served as chairman for twenty-six years, but he was involved in operations only briefly in the beginning and turned over management to a CEO. He is humble and often seeks advice from other board members. He always looks to improve his board governance skills. The continuity from this one good chair serving for a long period of time benefits the organization greatly. It is not a given that he will always be the chair; he stands for reelection every year. The organization has had an outstanding CEO for the last sixteen years and has experienced high growth in serving more clients living in poverty as well as revenue growth every year even through three recessions.

The working relationship between the chair and the CEO/ED is so effective because each adheres to his unique responsibilities.

BOARD TERM LIMITS

Be sure to have term limits for all board members other than the founders. Having founders on the board long term is a strong protection against mission drift. The first term of a new director should be only one year. This way, if they are not a fit, they can opt not to stand for reelection, or the board nominating committee can choose not to nominate that person for a second term.

Having an initial term of only one year might make it easier to attract highly capable board members, as they can easily exit in a short period of time. At Edify, the second and third terms are three years each. Some boards allow three two-year terms after the initial one-year term. The board member must then step off the board for at least one year. Be sure not to create an expectation that the same person will automatically be elected again. You should compare that person with other prospective candidates a year later. Always look to upgrade your board. Sometimes directors who are excellent at helping you in an early stage are not the best people to help you grow through later stages.

BOARD QUALITY IS CRUCIAL

Your board will either propel you forward or hinder your growth. From the first board member, pick each one with great care, using a board skill map. (See a board skill map at thesocialentrepreneur.org/tools.) As founding CEO/ED, you do not get to appoint board members other than the first one or two after you. However, it is your responsibility to speak up when the board begins to consider someone who is not an excellent fit. Take a leading role in suggesting candidates for chairman, the most influential board member. Go to great lengths to ensure that all who are appointed chair have extensive governance experience and will exercise best governance practices. Confirm with the candidate that they will intervene when a board member crosses the line into management's purview of running day-to-day operations and hiring and firing staff.

8

BEING A TRANSFORMATIONAL SOCIAL ENTREPRENEUR

TRANSFORMATIONAL LEADERS CAST exciting visions, inspire stakeholders, innovate solutions, and exponentially scale impact. Transformational leadership implies that a better desired future exists. There are two elements of transformational leadership: transforming the lives of those you serve and transforming how your organization serves them. The quest to be a transformational leader is an ongoing pursuit.

TRANSFORMING THOSE YOU SERVE

Imagine looking back on your life and seeing a trail of thousands of people and families whose lives were transformed because of your entrepreneurial efforts, which were powered by the Spirit of God. If you follow the principles below, you can be a transformational leader, building a great organization that is designed to dramatically transform the lives of many people.

Design your strategy around life transformation. There is a big difference between meeting a need in a person's life and actually transforming it.

If you want to be a transformational leader, you will need to be a student of human transformation.

Life change happens slowly over time and often requires several surrounding factors to be sustainable. Based on the target audience you desire to serve, what life transformation do you hope to see and measure when your work is done? What are the critical success factors that are most likely to enable that?

For example, at the Halftime Institute we learned early on that one-day events did not produce sustained life change. That kind of change needs a combination of process, peers, case studies, and one-on-one coaching. So we stopped doing one-day inspirational events because they didn't produce the life transformation that we desired. This allowed us to focus on the areas that yield greater impact and mission fulfillment.

At Edify, we saw that hundreds of thousands of good Christian schools educating children living in poverty in developing nations grew slowly because they did not have access to loans to expand their schools as rapidly as they desired. They were also hungry for better school management practices.

Seek the Lord for the right strategy, tactics for implementing the strategy, and passionate staff and board members who have the skills needed. (Please see the board skill map mentioned in Chapter 7 as well as how to choose and work with great mentors in Chapter 11.) Develop a theory of change (theoryofchange.org/what-is-theory-of-change).

Listen for the Holy Spirit's leading. Having a strategy for transforming lives is an important first step, but avoid being so rigid that you miss the leading of the Holy Spirit. If you instill the daily disciplines into your schedule that enable you to stay close to the Lord through prayer, Bible study, praise, and meditation, you will sense the Holy Spirit's leading. He may lead you on unexpected paths which you do not understand. He will reveal what you need to know at the right time as you build the habit of obeying His promptings.

As your prayer life becomes clearer to your staff, they will have more confidence and trust in your decisions. For example, God said of Caleb: "But because my servant Caleb has a different spirit and follows me wholeheartedly, I will bring him into the land he went to, and his descendants will inherit it" (Num. 14:24). Later, Caleb asked Joshua for permission to invade the land where the Israelites had failed to drive out the inhabitants. Caleb succeeded on this tough assignment where others had failed. In like manner, you can overcome great challenges by wholeheartedly following the Lord.

Dream about the transformational vision and mission to which God will lead you. Seek the Lord for His vision. Often His vision is much larger than you think possible. Be encouraged by this. Who wants to pursue a vision so small that you can achieve it on your own? Pursue a vision that can succeed only with the Lord's help. Here are three steps we have found helpful as you lean into the vision you feel God is giving you.

Work at casting the vision well. Write out and practice presenting the vision so it is compelling and emotional. You should appeal to people's logic and hearts as you explain that you seek to solve a big problem, you have an excellent solution to the problem, and you have assembled a strong entrepreneurial team to make it happen. Get coaching on the words you use and how you say them, including tone, hand gestures, and graphics used in the presentation. The Ardent Mentoring portal may have mentors who can advise you well on this.[22] Business school professors who teach entrepreneurship are often available for a fee to consult with you on this. If you have friends who have obtained venture capital or angel financing or provide such funding, they can help you make your pitch compelling and emotional. As you improve your ability to cast the vision, you will get real-time feedback about how well it resonates with both those you desire to serve and those you will need to help you.

Get wise advice. "Plans fail for lack of counsel, but with many advisers they succeed" (Prov. 15:22). Find people who have successfully grown from the current stage of your organization to the next several stages. If your organization is still young, look to entrepreneurs for advice rather than people who worked at large companies, who might not be able to relate well to your entrepreneurial challenges.

Be courageous. God told Joshua, "Be bold and strong! Banish fear and doubt!" (Josh. 1:9, TLB). After the Lord gives you the vision, pursue it with great confidence and energy. Be enthusiastic, even though the vision and challenges ahead are daunting. Have the courage to stop doing "good" things that don't produce the life transformation God calls you toward.

TRANSFORMING HOW YOUR ORGANIZATION SERVES

A few ingredients are essential to building an organization that is continuously being transformed to better serve your audience. We believe these are disciplines you can instill into your daily work habits and routines.

Build trust. Trust is an essential ingredient to allow your staff, management, and board to innovate and transform rather than becoming distracted by doubt. Trust is of great importance and should influence all that you say and do. If you answer a question or make a statement, be honest. Earning and maintaining the trust of your staff, board members, and donors is crucial in being a transformational leader. For example, when a staff member is dismissed for poor performance reasons, do not allow HR or the person's manager or yourself to put out an email praising that person. Staff members likely know the person was not performing well. Instead, say something like, "John Smith is no longer with us, and we wish him well in his next position."

Also, do not conceal significant negative information from your board of directors, your direct reports, and major donors. Because later, if you must reveal it or it becomes known from another source, the information comes as a big surprise. You will lose their trust if you did not disclose a big problem early. For example, suppose things are going badly in an area and the CEO/ED opts not to disclose the problem at the

> YOU WILL LOSE THEIR TRUST IF YOU DID NOT DISCLOSE A BIG PROBLEM EARLY.

next board meeting for fear of looking bad or in hopes that the problem can be turned around in the future. Instead, the problem gets worse, and the board and donors realize that the CEO/ED concealed the problem. They lose trust in the CEO/ED because they were not straightforward. They question the CEO/ED's willingness to seek advice when needed, as they could have given the CEO/ED ideas that would have solved the problem early.

Walt Rakowich, who ran the large international logistics and real estate company Prologis, wrote a book called *Transfluence: How to Lead with Transformative Influence in Today's Climates of Change*. It is about building trust in leadership and touches on the importance of overcoming fear and pride, acting with transparency and authenticity, embodying a strong set of values, and bringing passion and purpose to leadership. Rakowich says, "When leaders do these things, they can better build trust and enhance their opportunity to make their organizations and communities better."[23]

Genuinely care for your staff. Treating others well will build trust. Take a genuine interest in caring for your staff and those you serve. Whenever you possibly can, listen to a staff member's feelings, challenges, and suggestions with undivided, patient attention. Sometimes this is a challenge during a hectic day. However, sincerely caring about your staff is key to long-term success.

For example, as a follower of Jesus, model and make sure each staff member can take at least one full day off each week to rest or spend time with family. This will often be Sunday but could be a different day depending on the demands upon the organization. Your staff will be rejuvenated, and their families will be happier. Ask staff to come into the office on Saturdays only if truly necessary. This should be a rare occasion.

Treating others well results in mutual trust. My CFO at Comps InfoSystems was very patient and understanding. Because of her genuineness and kind manner, she was the most trusted executive in the company. The trust that people had in her often resulted in her being able to solve personal friction among employees when other executives could not. Trust will help you make the most of good opportunities and weather times of trouble.

Manage finances carefully. An old saying in business is "The first rule of entrepreneurship is never run out of cash." If you run out of cash, you will not be able to honor commitments and pay your staff. This is an existential threat. Budget expenses carefully month by month for the subsequent two years, and make sure you always have enough cash to meet those expenses. Build up several months of a cash cushion so you can weather temporary drops in donations/revenues. Such preparation helped many social enterprises get through the great recession of 2008–2009 and the pandemic of 2020–2022. Meet with your CFO or controller or bookkeeper monthly to compare your budget/projection to actual results.

Create a meritocracy of ideas. Go with the idea that best withstands the vigorous challenges of executives, board members, and advisors, regardless of whom the idea comes from. "Best idea wins" is a core value at Edify. Before implementing an important decision, ask people for constructive criticism on how the agreed-upon "best approach" could be wrong. Develop this culture among executives and board members. Encourage healthy debate and challenges to your thinking. When Chris was an executive at a large microfinance organization, he and his executives and board concluded that the best way to serve people living in poverty was to convert nonprofit microfinance institutions into regulated banks. This would allow disadvantaged people to have a place to save their money, in addition to borrowing. They did not adequately challenge themselves as to how the decision could be wrong. After a couple of low-cost probes that were not particularly successful, we jumped headlong into converting many of our nonprofits into commercial banks. We did not grasp how complicated banks are to operate and how governments were inclined to increase regulations dramatically. Tremendous amounts of money were lost, and the survival of the organization was severely threatened.

Lloyd and I have learned that we definitely do not have all the good ideas. We have also learned that some of our ideas are bad, and we need our executives, board members, and donors to point out the problems.

Operate in resourceful, evaluative, maximizer mode (REMM), not pain avoidance mode (PAM). Decades ago, a major business publication, likely *Forbes* or *Fortune Magazine*, ran a story on researchers from a prestigious university studying CEOs and other senior leaders. The researchers assumed such high-level people would operate 99 percent of their time being resourceful, carefully evaluating alternatives, and maximizing situations for the best outcome. Wrong! They operated this way only half of the time, and the other half of the time they operated in pain avoidance mode. The researchers were shocked to find how often highly experienced executives would avoid uncomfortable or painful decisions, rather than acknowledging the problem and promptly making the uncomfortable change to maximize results.

When Chris finds that he is uncomfortable about something and not making a decision, he asks himself if he is in pain avoidance mode. Often, he is. Fortunately, most of the time, he decides to bite the bullet, go through the discomfort or pain, and make the best decision for the organization and the people they serve. Being respected is more important than being liked, and making decisions that please everyone is rarely possible.

> RESEARCHERS WERE SHOCKED TO FIND HOW OFTEN HIGHLY EXPERIENCED EXECUTIVES WOULD AVOID UNCOMFORTABLE OR PAINFUL DECISIONS, RATHER THAN ACKNOWLEDGING THE PROBLEM.

A typical example of operating in pain avoidance mode is not dismissing a staff member when you know the person should be let go. Almost always, the longer you wait, the worse it gets. Other staff may question your leadership if you do not act on a person who is obviously not a fit for your organization.

Guard confidentiality. Sometimes you will need to say, "No comment," or, "I have nothing to say on that issue at this time," or, "I'm not at liberty to say anything." Further, do not say, "I don't know anything about that," when you do. Be honest but more importantly, keep things confidential when it is important to do so. Breaching confidentiality can create many problems.

When I (Chris) was CEO of a publicly traded company, had I mentioned to one or a few people that we were in negotiations to acquire another company and had not first issued a press release declaring what was occurring, it would have been a violation of the inside trading/information law. In other words, it would have been unfair for certain people to know this inside information and possibly profit by trading in our stock at the expense of others.

During my tenure, we acquired thirteen other companies. My standard reply when people asked if we were in discussions to acquire a particular company was, "Whether we are in discussions to acquire a company or not, I never comment." I had to say this even in situations where we had never had a discussion regarding acquiring a particular company. In other words, if I always said no when we were not in discussions, the listener could read between the lines when I didn't say no.

Often at this for-profit company, as well as at social enterprise organizations I managed, we would be in a discussion regarding a strategic alliance, acquiring or merging with another company, a new partnership, or a significant donation. I always chose a code word for the organization with which the discussions were being held. Such code words were innocuous, such as "baseball," "archery," "cowboy," and "pitcher." If the other organization requested confidentiality, I would only tell the code words to those very few staff members who needed to know.

In one case, I received a phone call in 2004 from the assistant to the head of economic development for the Bill and Melinda Gates Foundation. She told me the head wished to speak with me about the foundation possibly entering the field of microfinance and making a grant to Opportunity International. She stressed that all discussions regarding this must be kept entirely confidential for my organization to be considered.

I naturally agreed and immediately chose a code word for the Gates Foundation. We scheduled the call. The executive director told me the foundation wanted to learn about microfinance by starting with grants to only five microfinance organizations. He said Opportunity International was one of the fifteen organizations on the Foundation's short list. If any word got out that we were being considered, then Opportunity International would no longer be eligible for such a grant.

To develop an excellent proposal, I needed to engage our senior vice president of programs. He was the only person I informed about the project until two things happened: we received word that we had been chosen to receive a grant and the Bill and Melinda Gates Foundation issued a press release on the grant. The first grant was $2.2 million, but over the next three years we received total commitments of an additional $30 million. It would have been a tragedy had confidentiality not been kept and we had missed out on $32.2 million in grants.

However, someone on staff realized that I used a codename and felt this meant I did not trust the staff. That person then raised their concern to HR. To some extent the accusation of not trusting staff was correct. I did not trust the several thousand staff members all to keep this important issue confidential, whether it might be intentionally or accidentally "leaked." At a staff meeting after press releases were issued on the matter, I explained that the foundation had made it very clear that taking steps to honor the confidentiality was a condition of the grant. I gave my word that it would be kept confidential, and I needed to take steps to honor my word for the ultimate benefit of the disadvantaged people we served. Maintaining confidences will serve you well.

> MAINTAINING CONFIDENCES WILL SERVE YOU WELL.

Be a lifelong learner. Identify webinars, online resources, books, blogs, courses, and conferences from which you can learn to improve your leadership skills and expertise in your field. Some virtual offerings are free or inexpensive, such as the free course from Harvard Business School on entrepreneurship in emerging economies.[24]

You can take weeklong courses at Harvard Business School, such as Strategic Perspectives in Nonprofit Management, Performance Measurement for Effective Management of Nonprofit Organizations, or Governing for Nonprofit Excellence: Critical Issues for Board Leadership.[25]

Obtaining admission to these executive education courses at Harvard and other prestigious universities with similar offerings is much easier and less time-consuming than programs that grant degrees at those universities. Also, numerous universities have inexpensive courses as well as one-day and two-day conferences on nonprofit management.

Stanford publishes the *Stanford Social Innovation Review*,[26] reporting on many innovations by social entrepreneurs, and Harvard Business School has a Social Enterprise Initiative with numerous resources available.[27]

By applying the principles in this chapter for transforming the lives of others through transformational leadership in your organization, your efforts will result in profound and long-lasting transformation for many people. Please remember that your ongoing personal transformation through spiritual growth from prayer, Scripture reading, godly advice, and being led by the Holy Spirit is the most important part of your transformational leadership and ability to achieve 100x impact. Also, integral to long-term transformational leadership and impact is adhering to your mission, as we will see in the next chapter.

9

STAYING TRUE TO MISSION

ENSURING THAT CURRENT and future team members stay true to your mission is extremely important when building your team.

An organization's long-term impact is on the mind of all founders desiring to leave a legacy bigger than themselves. All too often the mission of an organization drifts from the founder's intent to the priorities of future leaders, with the risk of mission drift occurring with each generation of leaders.

After working long and hard to build your organization, think of the disappointment you would feel looking back when you are old and seeing your organization having drifted from its mission, perhaps even pursuing a mission antithetical to your values. Optimizing the probability that your organization will stay true to its mission takes intentionality. Careful planning, instituting guardrails, and consistent oversight are just some of the ways organizations stay on course. Leading expert on staying true to mission, Becca Spradlin, the founder of On Mission, said to me in an interview for this book, "To be clear, innovation and adaptation over time are to be expected for any organization. Therefore, it is critical for founders to define what is and is *not* mission drift for their organizations."[28]

History shows that drifting from mission is woefully common. This usually occurs one small degree at a time. Board members or executives who are not fully aligned with the mission join the organization. Perhaps some seemingly minor changes to language in your mission statement or values are made. Other times a significant contribution is accepted from a misaligned donor or investor. Over time, their grants or investments add restrictions that require watering down the mission. This all can happen with great subtlety—like the frog in the kettle not realizing the water keeps getting hotter.

Staying true to mission is the CEO/ED's and the board's highest responsibility for any organization that seeks to operate beyond the tenure of the founder. Donors have given money because of your mission, sometimes for decades. That trust should be rewarded with honesty, integrity, and faithfulness to remain true to the mission they funded. Please honor your donors' intentions.

One critical step to remain on mission is to enshrine the most important elements of your work in your bylaws. They can act as guardrails to keep present and future CEOs/EDs and boards true to the core mission. In the first section of its bylaws, Edify states the following:

> The primary purpose of Edify is to proclaim Jesus Christ and develop Christian character in students, teachers, and school staff. We will seek to speak about/or model the love of Jesus in each interaction with other people and do so in a culturally sensitive manner. Notwithstanding anything to the contrary herein, this primary purpose of proclaiming Jesus Christ cannot be changed unless there are unanimous votes of 100% of all then duly elected members of the Edify Board of Directors at face-to-face meetings in three consecutive years. In other words, changing this primary purpose shall take no less than three full years to do, and there must be at least one face-to-face, in-person, board meeting, not videoconference, not teleconference, not consent minutes, in each of three consecutive years attended by 100% of the then elected Directors, not just a quorum, at each of said three meetings, at which all elected Directors unanimously vote to change this primary purpose.

Chris thanks Wess Stafford for helping plan from the very start to avoid mission drift. Wess, then CEO of Compassion International, called one day and said, "Hey, Chris. I hear you've started a new organization. What's the primary goal?"

I said, "It's to impart Christ-centered character in children."

"Isn't your goal to make a lot of loans to schools?"

"That's part of it, but it's not the main goal."

"Is it to improve academic education?" he pressed.

"We're interested in that, but our number-one goal is children coming to the saving knowledge of Jesus Christ and becoming leaders who share Jesus with others."

"That's great, Chris," Wess said. "But thirty years from now, when you're gone, how are you going to be sure that Edify's future board or management will stick to that? Given how many organizations eventually drift from their founding focus?"

"Wess, we just filed the nonprofit papers to get started," I told him. "We haven't even thought about thirty years down the road. But since you're asking the question, I bet you have."

He told me Compassion had a bylaw in its charter that can't be changed except by a unanimous vote of all the directors—not just a quorum or not just all board directors at a particular meeting. This was Compassion's way to keep their board successors from drifting from the mission.

Before a new executive is hired or a new board member is appointed, make sure they are fully aligned with your primary mission and passionate about it. Otherwise, they might make decisions or push for policies that are out of alignment with your mission.

Becca Spradlin stated:

> "It is important that new leaders are not just passive accepters of the mission but are enthusiastic champions, whom you can trust to strengthen and advance the core of your work."[29]

Every time a social enterprise goes through a CEO/ED transition or a board chair transition, risk of mission drift heightens. The search committee recruiting for those positions should immediately eliminate anyone not passionate about the primary mission. Otherwise, the door is open to drift.

The time to implement guardrails to avoid mission drift is when the board thinks drift will never occur. Case after case proves that this scenario is a false sense of security. Implement guardrails when everyone is in agreement with the mission and will vote to codify it in the bylaws. Do this early, and do not wait. Boards confident that drift will not happen are often surprised ten or twenty years later when new board members seek to change the mission.

Influence on the mission will come not only from future board members and executives but also from your donors. Peter Greer, CEO of HOPE International, along with Chris Horst, VP at HOPE, wrote the excellent book *Mission Drift*. They emphasize the importance of taking money only from like-minded donors. Large donors with missions different than yours are likely the most frequent cause of organizations engaging in mission drift. Here are some quotes from Greer and Horst's book:

- "Mission True organizations recruit and engage Mission True donors."
- "Yet as we read and heard stories of Mission Drift, we were surprised how often corporate, government, and foundation donors drove the drift. Organizations compromised on their core values to woo these institutional funders."
- "Donors are an accurate predictor of whether an organization is going to deviate off mission. Donors either center an organization on its full mission or contribute to Mission Drift."[30]

Some of the largest Christian organizations assisting people living in poverty started out also sharing Jesus. However, over time, many failed to continue sharing the saving knowledge of Christ. An example is ChildFund, originally founded as China Children's Fund in 1938 by Presbyterian minister J. Calvitt Clarke. In 1951 the organization took the name Christian Children's Fund. Chris had a conversation on June 25, 2003, with the then CEO. When Chris asked how Christian Children's Fund expressed Christianity in their work, the CEO said the organization was then Christian in name only. In 2010, the name was changed to ChildFund with the following explanation: "It was a rebranding that served as a springboard to a new strategy to enhance supporter engagement and the organization's programs for children."[31] Wikipedia says, "Some criticized the organization for appearing to be a Christian organization long after it had ended its religious affiliation."[32]

I am sad when I see long-time Christian organizations depart from their roots.

For some, drifting from mission happened when they decided to accept government or corporate or secular foundation grants. This led to no longer combining the Great Commission with the Great Commandment (loving God and loving your neighbor as you love yourself). It is easy to fall into the trap of saying, "If we downplay our faith, we will be able to raise more money to help more people." Often such organizations drifted from their original mission after the founders no longer had significant involvement. It is important to note, as stated in Chapter 2, that staying true to a mission of proclaiming Jesus can actually result in more contributions, not fewer. It's sad: nonaligned donations resulting in drifting from mission often amount to only 10–20 percent of the organization's entire revenues. It is a tragic turn to pursue a small increase in revenues that results in an organization losing its soul and drifting from its carefully crafted original mission.

> IT IS A TRAGIC TURN TO PURSUE A SMALL INCREASE IN REVENUES THAT RESULTS IN AN ORGANIZATION LOSING ITS SOUL.

Worse yet, seemingly small changes to placate some donors may backfire by turning off your core, committed donor base. Chris saw a Christian social enterprise pursue large corporate grants, which eventually required downplaying Jesus, and lose 50 percent of its revenues in just four years. It was still at that low point nine years later.

It is helpful to have tools to indicate the degree of risk in accepting a donation. Friends of ours run a nonprofit helping disadvantaged young people navigate their way into a productive adulthood. Organization staff often share their Christian faith. They have developed a matrix with "Donor Alignment" (see quadrant graph below) as the vertical line and "Donor Pressure" as the horizontal line. Pressure includes terms of the grant contract, percent of annual revenues, influence the grantor staff attempts to exert, and the burden of reporting. If the donor falls in the upper left quadrant (high alignment and low pressure), it receives a green light. If they plot the donor near the center of the graph, the nonprofit takes extra caution when applying for or accepting such a grant. If the donor falls in the lower right quadrant (high pressure and low alignment), grants from such donors are not pursued or accepted.

DONOR MISSION ALIGNMENT/PRESSURE ANALYSIS

MISSION ALIGNMENT (HIGH)

	Low Pressure	High Pressure
High Alignment	**Seek** — Highly aligned donors who trust management on how best to use the money.	**Be Cautious Of** — Aligned but activist donors seeking partial strategy change.
Low Alignment	**Watch Closely** — Less aligned donors who don't desire to influence your strategy.	**Avoid** — Poorly aligned donors with an activist agenda.

DONOR PRESSURE (LOW → HIGH)

Be especially circumspect of government grants. The apostle Paul warns, "Don't team up with those who are unbelievers" (2 Cor. 6:14, NLT). The motives behind government grants shift depending on the ambitions of current politicians, the issues they face, or what will bring them personal political gain. If such personal gain comes from shutting down a Christian nonprofit that took government grants, aggressive state attorneys generals have done so. An example is when the Pennsylvania attorney general sued Catholic Social Services for its adoption policy of not placing children with single parents or homosexual couples but only with married, heterosexual couples. The attorney general sued even though 60 percent of placements were minority children with minority families, and no homosexuals had ever applied to Catholic Social Services to adopt a child. Another example is when the nun order Little Sisters of the Poor was sued for exercising their First Amendment right to freedom of religion by refusing to provide abortion pills to their staff in their work of serving the poor. Both Christian organizations lost in the lower courts. The US Supreme Court had to step in and overturn those rulings and restore the freedom of religion rights of the two organizations to continue serving disadvantaged people.

Government grants almost always come with strings. Sometimes those strings are contained not in the document your organization signed with the government but some current or future state or federal law of which you are totally unaware. You may wish to write in your bylaws that your organization will never accept any kind of government funding unless a supermajority of 75 percent or 100 percent of the board members vote to do so. Edify opted for a 100 percent supermajority as its threshold. That is a true supermajority!

Is your trust in the Lord sufficient to accept money only from like-minded donors? Proverbs 3:5–6 states: "Trust in the LORD with all your heart; do not depend on your own understanding. Seek his will in all you do, and he will show you which path to take" (NLT). Mother Teresa said she preferred "the insecurity of divine providence."[33]

Many people say if you remove the name of Jesus or God from your website and marketing materials, you will raise more money because your potential donor base expands. As we mentioned, when Chris became CEO of Opportunity International, it was one of the three largest US-based organizations conducting microfinance in developing countries. All three organizations had similar revenues. Seven years later, Opportunity had more revenue than the other two organizations combined, even though they were secular and Opportunity International emphasized Jesus in its materials. There is a significant possibility that you will raise more money by emphasizing Jesus instead of attempting to appeal to a larger audience by deemphasizing God.

> *"Therefore, my dear brothers and sisters, stand firm. Let nothing move you. Always give yourselves fully to the work of the Lord, because you know that your labor in the Lord is not in vain." (1 Cor. 15:58)*

Becca Spradlin of On Mission performs a "Mission True Audit" every two years for Edify. These findings are reported directly to the Mission True subcommittee of the Edify board governance committee and then the entire board. We find this to be an invaluable safeguard for staying true to mission—not only for the leadership but for the staff, who are also interviewed during the audit process. Below are thoughts from Becca Spradlin:

> We encourage leadership teams to think through how they might define, protect, and champion their mission, particularly the Christ-centered elements of their work or desired impact. Using this framework, we quickly find that an often overlooked yet simple step to avoiding mission drift is defining what it looks like to stay on mission. Leaders and boards can do significant good by taking an hour or two across several meetings to define drift. From there, they can protect the core of their mission by articulating it in governing documents, job advertisements, websites, marketing materials or other outlets. Hiring for mission fit is essential at all levels. Leaders must continually emphasize

the core of the mission throughout the year to embed it in the culture and with their board. These regular practices of defining, discussing, and reiterating the core mission help cultivate internal and external champions of the mission. This greatly increases the likelihood of staying on mission for generations of leaders to come.[34]

Infuse your mission into every dimension of your strategic plan. Ensure that every strategic initiative and tactic of your strategic plan is in full accord with your mission. Have a "True North" metric through which every significant decision is run. We believe this will help you multiply your impact now and long into the future, hopefully 100x. Edify's metric is "Will this decision help disciple and educate more children better?" Combine this chapter's recommendations with the next chapter's recommendations on incorporating wisdom into your social enterprise efforts.

> INFUSE YOUR MISSION INTO EVERY DIMENSION OF YOUR STRATEGIC PLAN.

PART 3

ADVICE FOR BEING A SUCCESSFUL SOCIAL ENTREPRENEUR

10

EFFECTIVE FUNDRAISING

OBTAINING THE NECESSARY funding to scale your organization is critical whether you are running a for-profit social enterprise or nonprofit. Some social entrepreneurs, for-profit or nonprofit, can sell their services or products at a sufficient price so that all expenses are covered shortly after opening their doors. Chris once knew a software engineer who had started a company with just enough money to hire a few other software developers for several months. They quickly developed a good-enough software product and were selling enough each month to cover all expenses. The entrepreneur said he would rather spend time selling the product than taking months to pursue venture capitalists, who may or may not invest in his company. The strategy worked well for him as his company became quite successful. Later, he and his key executives ended up owning 100 percent of the company. They could make the best decisions for their company without the pressure of doing a liquidity event based on the timing needs of an outside investor.

Some of the Christian school entrepreneurs Chris serves use money they save plus some money borrowed from friends and family to build several classrooms. They then market the new school by knocking on doors in the community and soon gain enough students to be financially sustainable in just a few weeks or months after opening day.

When Lloyd started Halftime Institute's work in the Carolinas as a social enterprise to serve successful business leaders in those two states, he intentionally designed the launch to require no upfront capital and very few fixed costs. As a result, they've had positive cash flow every year for more than a decade. With some careful thought, you might be able to do this with your social enterprise.

Most social entrepreneurs must raise money from investors or donors. This means putting together a compelling value proposition and identifying prospective funders. Sophisticated funders will often ask those challenging questions that make you a better entrepreneur with a more refined strategy. You should obtain mentoring from entrepreneurs who have been successful in raising money, ideally several times before.

Sophisticated investors and donors may use a formula such as:

Valuation = Problem x Solution x Leverage x Entrepreneurial Team

Valuation. This is the amount of money your company is worth or the attractiveness for your nonprofit to receive a donation. Sophisticated philanthropists will gauge how much impact they can have with a donation to you as compared to another organization. Will more lives be transformed through your efforts than competing proposals they receive?

Problem. Are you pursuing a big need? If you have a terrific cure for a disease, but only one hundred people in the world have the disease, it is a small problem other than for the few persons afflicted. Are there many other organizations attempting to solve the problem you have identified, thus making the problem likely to be solved eventually without you?

> WILL IT LEAD TO SYSTEMIC CHANGE TO SOLVE THE PROBLEM?

Solution. Is your solution more effective and much lower in cost than existing solutions? Is it a disruptive innovation—a breakthrough in solving the problem? Will it lead to systemic change to solve the problem nationally, internationally, or globally? Will you share your successful methodology with many others interested in this problem, so that maximum effort can be made toward a solution? Is it patented or otherwise proprietary, resulting in barriers to entry from competitors? What is the cost per person benefited in the next year and three years from now? Is the solution scalable? Have you minimized risks of failure as much as you reasonably can? Can you develop a minimal viable product to determine acceptance in the market inexpensively and quickly? Have you conducted a low-cost probe indicating the effectiveness of your solution? Are you doing a lean startup to minimize costs until, and even after, you gain traction with your product or service?

Leverage. Will you partner with other organizations or use other resources to scale much more rapidly at much less cost? When Chris cofounded Edify, he and cofounder Tiger Dawson decided never to build a school to be operated by Edify. Rather, they found that hundreds of thousands of Christian schools had already been started by local social entrepreneurs. The schools often had three hundred or more children. They decided to help existing schools improve Christian discipleship of students, build more classrooms, improve academic education, and offer education technology. Edify partnered with local Christian microfinance institutions that were licensed lenders to make loans to these schools to build classrooms, repair roofs, purchase computer labs, purchase vans to transport children to school, etc. Thus, Edify did not need licenses to make loans in each of its twelve countries of operations, did not have to hire bankers to set up lending branches, and did not have to collect loan repayments. The local Christian microfinance institutions did all this. And the repayment rate was much higher with locals working for a well-known local institution collecting the monthly installments than Americans trying to do so.

Edify seeks to avoid developing/building anything new, if it can find a service or system already in existence that is almost as good or better. If another organization, methodology, or software system can do the job 70 percent as well as if we develop it ourselves, we almost always go with what is already available.

Innovative social entrepreneurs can often find numerous ways to leverage their organization and supporters' donations. Chris and his Edify cofounder leveraged the existing infrastructure of Christian schools in developing nations with existing microfinance institutions that only needed to be made aware of the opportunity to loan to schools, along with much free, educational, Christian content that could be easily adapted. One major donor told Chris and Tiger that he never funded startup ministries. However, he was willing to fund Edify early. He said, "You're not a startup. All you are doing is assembling parts that are already there and already work." Effective use of leverage will multiply your impact many times over.

Entrepreneurial Team. This is the most important variable in the equation. Savvy investors and philanthropists will ask themselves if the CEO/ED has founded and scaled an organization before. Were some of the current management team members part of that successful scaleup? Does the team have the skills and track record to indicate that they will be successful in scaling the enterprise?

Many social entrepreneurs have few or none of the preceding elements of the equation but are still successful. They typically have a great vision and can cast it in a compelling manner, or they may partially compensate for their lack of experience by having successful entrepreneurs on their board of directors or as executives. However, it is easier for the funder to have confidence in managers who have been successful entrepreneurs before. The entrepreneurial team gets a double weighting in the formula when each of the four variables are multiplied by each other. Therefore, if you as a CEO/ED have limited successful operating experience, then recruit executives, board members, and mentors who bring these valuable skills.

CEO/ED AS FUNDRAISER

The CEO/ED is critical to fundraising during the early stages, when they are likely the only one raising funds. In the middle and later stages when there are numerous full-time fundraisers, the CEO/ED may participate primarily in important donor/investor visits in the late stages of a donation/investment request. This is when donors want to look the CEO/ED in the eye for assurance that the funds will be used properly before they write a six- or seven-figure check. The CEO/ED will always need to be heavily involved in fundraising, unless you have a remarkably successful marketing campaign to mass-market donors rather than major donors.

Hire a consultant to help with fundraising presentations. When you raise funds, find a consultant who can help you with your presentation in terms of content, delivery, and graphics. An excellent consultant can make a dramatic difference in the effectiveness of your presentation. When Chris took his company public through an IPO, the investment banker required him to meet with a presentation consultant before starting a three-week trip to make ninety presentations to 170 institutional investment companies on two continents.

Chris had made many presentations on his company in the past and thought his presentation was already very good, with little need for a consultant. He was amazed at how the consultant pointed out weaknesses, gaps, distracting hand gestures, lackluster graphics, and a lack of effective modulation and pauses for effect. He realized his presentation was not "very good" but rather merely fair. After making the consultant's suggested changes, Chris hit the road with a greatly improved presentation, which led to a successful IPO. Thus, a good presentation consultant can mean the difference between your organization raising significant donations and scaling rapidly or smaller donations and impacting far fewer people.

Shortly after joining a microfinance organization, a caring venture philanthropist offered to have the presentation consultant he kept on retainer work with Chris to improve his presentation. Chris immediately accepted, knowing the benefits of such a critique.

Avoid the $500,000–$2 million trap. Many nonprofits get stuck for years or decades in a box of raising between $500,000–$2 million (in 2022 US dollar purchasing power). This is often because the executive director spends their time managing programs as well as doing all the fundraising. The board may have mandated that general and administrative expenses plus fundraising expenses not exceed 20 percent of total revenues. Thus, the executive director does not have the budget to hire a fundraiser.

> MANY NONPROFITS GET STUCK RAISING BETWEEN $500,000–$2 MILLION.

This creates a trap, and the organization may never get out of this funding box. As a result, the executive director might never be able to see enough donors and manage the growing operations. Often, they will burn out. Another way of getting stuck in this trap is hiring fundraisers who fail. The time and expense of such repeated failures causes the organization to conclude that the best way forward is to rely solely on the CEO/ED for all fundraising. Rarely does this misguided decision lead to scaling and impacting many people.

We estimate that even the best nonprofit CEOs/EDs often select fundraisers who do not last more than two years with an organization. Shortly after starting Edify, Chris and his cofounder, Tiger Dawson, had three of their first four fundraiser hires fail. Chris and Tiger had hired many fundraisers in the past. Tiger asked, "How can we be so bad at this?" Fortunately, most of the subsequent fundraising hires worked out well, and Edify raised $11 million in its twelfth year of operation.

Institute a good recruiting process. Organizations usually rely on good processes to increase the chance of a good hire. Such tools will often include a carefully written job description; effective dissemination of the job description to good candidates; an executive recruiter; and an efficient system to sort good applicants from the rest and respond promptly and warmly to them. Evaluation tools, such as a weighting/rating template being used by every staff member every time they interview candidates, are critical. (Consult the endnotes for a sample template on weighting and rating.)[35] Organizing multiple interviews with the candidate, followed by the interview team discussing the candidate immediately after each round of interviews, is important.

A good recruiting process is a lot of work, but it is well worth it given that hiring decisions are among the most important decisions an organization makes.

Engaging a psychologist who regularly screens salespeople and fundraisers can significantly increase your successful recruiting rate as well. The psychologist may ask to profile your most successful fundraisers, which will allow for identifying attributes that work well raising money for your organization and its mission. Chris had a friend who had hired hundreds of salespeople during his career. That friend always used a sales psychologist and said that every time he went against the psychologist's recommendation, it turned out to be a mistake. Of course, he referred to the psychologist only candidates who had made it through several interviews. Hiring is such an important decision. We recommend involving people highly experienced in effective recruiting, including psychologists when it comes to fundraisers or salespeople.

If you do not have a good recruiting process, you're likely to end up with a low-performing team, serve far fewer people, and have less personal joy. Get a good system in place. It is like the adage "If you fail to plan, you are planning to fail."

Hire good fundraisers. Hiring productive fundraisers who will stay with you for five or more years is a big challenge that you need to overcome. Many fundraisers change jobs every two years. That person will likely be a net negative to your organization! You will have spent much time with them with donors, paid them a salary and benefits, and they likely will not have raised as much money as you have paid them. Your time will have been wasted, and their departure will be disruptive to the donors assigned to them. Do not hire job hoppers who have a track record of changing fundraising jobs every two or three years. Regardless of how much they tell you that they really want to stay long term at your organization, their actions speak more loudly than their words. Do not hire them!

Seek to hire fundraisers who are in the top 10 percent of all fundraisers, and then pay them accordingly. When I (Chris) started as CEO of Opportunity International, I asked to see the amount of money each fundraiser was raising as well as their cost in terms of salary, bonus, benefits, travel, and home-office support. Some were raising only twice their expenses. If they had been with the organization less than three years, this was okay. However, for those who had been with the organization four years or more, it was reasonable to expect each of them to be raising 3x to 10x their expenses. I discovered that we had some fundraisers who were raising 20x their expenses but were only paid 30 percent more than those raising 5x. I changed that.

Some of the outstanding fundraisers had children starting college soon. Their salaries wouldn't be sufficient to cover two or three children in college or graduate school at the same time. I significantly raised the compensation of those raising 10x their overall expense. I did this for two reasons. First, it was fair given their great performance. Second, it would avoid their showing up in my office one day saying they had accepted a fundraising position with another organization because they would receive the $25,000–$50,000 more per year needed to fund their children's education. It is terribly expensive to lose a person raising $2–$4 million annually. Instead, proactively raising their compensation by $50,000–$100,000 per year is much better.

Both organizations that I worked for abided by the rules of the Association of Fundraising Professionals: "[It is] permitted to accept [pay] performance-based compensation, such as bonuses, only if such bonuses are in accordance with prevailing practices within the members' own organizations and are not based on a percentage of contributions."[36] For example, if a fundraiser far exceeded expectations regarding donations to the organization, they earned a bonus. That bonus was in no way a percentage of funds raised. It was based on numerous factors, such as the difficulty of their territory, the effort they made, the courage they exhibited by pursuing many new donors, significantly increasing funds raised with their existing donors, and overall level of funds raised during the year. I also looked at how good of a team player they were when making referrals to other fundraisers in other territories, mentoring new fundraisers, and referring prospective fundraisers for us to hire. Their expense ratio was also considered: What were their expenses per dollar raised? Carefully managing expenses and raising high donations could merit a bonus.

There was not a formula; it was more of an art than a science.

Another part of the bonus was a promotion and a new title. Typically, fundraisers raising over $2 million per year for three or more years were promoted to vice president. They were *not* corporate vice presidents, and they often still had no employees reporting to them (except for star fundraisers who had full-time assistants). The other fundraisers typically shared one assistant among four fundraisers. Sometimes the title of vice president helped them raise even more money. It was important to make clear that if they received the vice president title, it did not mean that they were senior executives who would attend senior management team meetings.

Get lots of advice from board members and others who have successfully hired fundraisers and salespeople. Involve those advisors in the interview process. This will help you avoid many poor hires and attract the outstanding performers you need. (Consult the endnotes for a template Edify uses to assist in evaluating fundraisers.)[37]

Assembling a great team of long-term fundraisers can propel your organization to far greater heights than settling for a group of mediocre fundraisers, many of whom will stay with you for only a couple of years. Invest in those who will provide the majority of the financial resources necessary to transform the lives of many more people, and then you will be on the path to 100x impact. Good mentors, as you'll see in the next chapter, can also be invaluable in recruiting high performers for your enterprise.

11

CHOOSING AND USING GREAT MENTORS

IF YOU HAVE great people on your team, little else matters. If you don't have great people, little else matters. Caring and knowledgeable mentors both for you and your top leaders can make the difference between transforming the lives of far more people or far fewer. Mentors can help you best take advantage of opportunities that catapult your mission forward and avoid pitfalls that could set you back years.

If it were not for Chris's mentor, Merrill Oster, encouraging him to buy the company he did and providing invaluable insights to turn the business around, Chris's life would have been very different. Also, when others told Chris not to assume the CEO role at Opportunity International to do microfinance in twenty-eight developing nations, Merrill gave Chris the encouragement that prompted his journey into social entrepreneurship.

Often Chris would call Merrill for advice and say, "Here's the problem, and here's what I'm thinking about doing to solve it."

Merrill would respond, "Yeah, that is what I did the first time I had that problem, and it didn't work. Here's what I did the second, third, and fourth time that resolved the problem."

> *Outstanding, Christ-centered mentors are available for Christian social entrepreneurs with a compelling vision to transform the lives of many people.*

But you must identify them, persuade them to mentor you, obtain the most important advice you can, and show that you value them with your actions.

Get very clear on the criteria for selecting your mentors: what your desired outcomes are, why their specific expertise is so important to you, and how long you expect to need their help. As you define criteria to pick a mentor, keep in mind that the best mentors are wise, caring, humble, empathetic, discreet, good listeners, encouraging, and advise from a biblical worldview. You will do well to compare all advice received with biblical principles to ensure they are in accord.

Make a short list of prospective mentors, rank them based on your criteria, and then contact them for a meeting. You don't need to say that you wish them to mentor you. Rather, it is fine to say that you are seeking advice on a particular challenge. When there is good chemistry, mentoring relationships naturally flow. If being bold and taking the first step of making contact is out of your comfort zone, relax. This is only one of very many times that you will have to get out of your comfort zone during your social entrepreneur journey. So, be bold! Be ready to provide the potential mentor with a thoughtful answer when they ask why you want their advice.

Some prospective mentors will agree to one initial session just to see how serious and competent you are. And unless you know the person well, starting with one session and seeing how you connect is probably wise. Carefully prepare for that first session by sending the mentor a concise description of your personal background, your organization, background information on the issues you wish to discuss, and an agenda. Be brief so you can be a good steward of their time.

If the initial session goes well, you might then ask for an additional four sessions, one per month, focused on achieving your stated goals. If all goes well, the sessions may continue and focus on different goals. Sometimes mentoring relationships go on for many years, touching base just once or twice per year after the initial twelve to twenty-four months.

If your mentor is open to more meetings, ask if you can provide them a summary of information before each meeting to optimize the next conversation. We suggest you offer to send the mentor five pieces of information in writing:

- Give a concise statement of the primary challenge you are facing, some background to help them understand the challenge, and your desired outcome.
- Describe how this issue is affecting you personally at an emotional level.
- Explain what you have tried so far and what the results were.
- Spell out the options that you see going forward.
- Detail what you would like from the mentor during the session.

The above will frame the discussion for the mentor so they can focus on solutions you have not considered as well as advise you on flaws that caused your earlier efforts not to prosper.

The best mentors want to invest their time in high-performing, committed people who will diligently consider the mentor's advice and use it effectively.

Good mentees do this by preparing carefully for meetings, taking good notes during the meetings, and reporting back which advice they are implementing and, later, the results. Good mentees also pray ahead of time for the meeting and the mentor.

Fred Smith, longtime executive director of The Gathering, an organization of very generous Christian donors learning from each other, wrote a blog post on what to look for in a mentor.[38]

HOW DO THE BEST MENTORS FIND PROSPECTIVE MENTEES?

Lloyd, who has invested 23,000 hours over the years coaching and mentoring high-capacity leaders, helped Chris develop criteria for evaluating prospective mentees. We share Chris's criteria below. Hopefully, these prompt ideas for you as you prepare for and present yourself to a prospective mentor:

1. Is the person involved in Christian social entrepreneurship?
2. Do they have high integrity, a high commitment to the social venture, and high potential to impact many people significantly? If so, will my time invested with this person yield a greater return in future years than if I spent the time on my own humanitarian work or a different mentee?
3. Is the entrepreneur truly passionate about serving others, or are they focused on personal achievement, winning awards, or other personal motives?
4. Does the entrepreneur's track record indicate that they are a high performer?
5. Has the entrepreneur already started an organization, which has been operating for a few years and overcome obstacles, thereby indicating that the person will persevere?
6. Will the entrepreneur take notes on the advice given, edit those notes, and email them to me so I have the notes to share with other Christian social entrepreneurs I mentor?
7. Is the entrepreneur combining the Great Commandment with the Great Commission?
8. Do my skills fill important gaps with other mentor(s) the mentee has? Can the entrepreneur show me a mentor skill map (see

thesocialentrepreneur.org/tools) they have made regarding the range of skills from the other mentor(s) they already have?
9. Is there a good reason to believe the mentee will seriously consider my advice and will implement some of my recommendations? As I work with the person, will there be evidence that they are implementing the recommendations we have agreed upon?
10. Is the entrepreneur regularly implementing a good plan to grow spiritually?
11. Will I learn much from the entrepreneur that will add value to my work with other social entrepreneurs as well as my social enterprise? Will my association with the entrepreneur's social venture provide me with input, perspective, and creative ideas?
12. Do I enjoy being with this person?
13. Is this person likely to share with others what I teach them? If so, then my efforts may be multiplied many times.

Lloyd has his own set of criteria for selecting mentees, in a more quantitative approach, using a rating template seeking scores of 8-5-8 based on the below:

- *Capability*: The person is 8 or above on a scale of 10 (with 10 being the highest) regarding the capability to achieve. Although the prospective mentee may be young, they should have a track record of achievement.
- *Clarity*: 5 or below in knowing how best to execute on their vision. This intentionally low score is important because Lloyd's core contribution is in the areas of vision and strategy. He is a thought leader, not an organizational leader. If the mentee has high clarity already, Lloyd may not be able to contribute as much value as usual.
- *Desire*: 8 or above regarding their desire to make a 100x impact with their life.

Lloyd makes an intuitive assessment of each of these three factors during the initial mentoring conversations. He asks a mentee to share their story, looking for indicators from their past regarding capability and follow-through. He asks questions about their vision, looking for indicators around clarity and scale. Perhaps the hardest to assess is their level of desire. For one young, single, current mentee, Lloyd set their monthly mentoring session at 8 a.m. on Saturday morning as a test of their true desire.

Lloyd and I each hope to mentor one hundred Christian social entrepreneurs over the next ten years. Hopefully, ten of those use our advice to make a huge difference in the trajectory of the number of people transformed. With medical advances in life longevity, many of the entrepreneurs will work an additional forty or fifty years.

If our advice helps them grow on average 5 percent more per year, this will likely result in tens of millions more people being transformed.

Thus, as Lloyd pointed out to me, this next decade may result in far more productivity than my prior forty-five years of working. Naturally, we each also hope to help our other ninety entrepreneur mentees grow faster than they would have without our mentoring.

Having several mentors at each stage of the growth of your organization is wise. One might help you in determining the sequential order of hiring key people. Another might help you with financial projections, strategy, developing low-cost probes and minimal viable products, another with building a fundraising team, and another with assembling a strong board. Further, mentors who give excellent advice in startup stages might not be the best advisors when your organization grows larger.

Do not be surprised if you receive conflicting advice from wise mentors with significant experience. Take what they have shared to the Lord to determine whose advice you will follow. Other times mentors may ask excellent questions rather than giving you specific advice. Famous management professor and author Peter Drucker said asking the right question is 50 percent of the solution.[39] If a mentor gives you constructive criticism, consider it a gift. Avoid being defensive. Very few people will honestly tell you the mistakes they see you making. Ask your mentors to be candid regarding criticism, and once you really understand their feedback ask additional questions to understand what they feel you should do next to address it. Thank them for the things they say that are hard to hear. As the Bible says, "Faithful are the wounds of a friend" (Prov. 27:6, KJV).

BEING A GREAT MENTEE

Lloyd and I have identified different types of mentees. Based on the descriptions below, which type of mentee do you currently resemble the most?

- *Diligent*: Earnestly seeks wise advice, carefully considers the advice given, and informs mentor of decisions and actions taken or planned regarding the advice. Comes to mentoring meetings on time and well prepared. Open to constructive criticism to become a better leader and identify blind spots. Makes notes of advice given during meeting, edits the notes, and sends to the mentor within forty-eight hours.
- *Busy*: Sincerely wishes to get good advice but is so busy that there is no time to carefully consider the advice given and act on it.
- *Casual*: Has heard that it is important to have a mentor but only wishes to hear good ideas and not make the effort to follow up on those ideas.
- *Presumptive*: Expects the mentor to take notes, edit them, and do the work that mentees should be doing for themselves.

- *Overly Confident*: Only wishes to be affirmed for having such a great idea or plan, and not interested in hearing of flaws, pitfalls, and misguided aspects of the plan.
- *Unfit*: Comes to meetings unprepared, sometimes arrives late or even misses meetings, and takes neither notes nor the mentoring relationship seriously.
- *Beginner*: So early in the process they are not ready for mentoring but rather should read books related to the field they wish to pursue.
- *Pre-Beginner*: Undecided regarding a field to pursue. Rather than taking up the time of an expert mentor, this person should likely take aptitude tests and, if young, speak with professors they had in college for advice. If forty years or older, they should speak with the Halftime Institute (halftimeinstitute.org).
- *Disinterested*: A board member or donor or other person required or pressured the person to receive mentoring against their will. There is little openness to making changes or new ideas.

RESOURCES TO BE A GREAT MENTEE

Great mentors like the late Rick Woolworth seek to "mentor entrepreneurs who will each have 100x impact or more." That's leverage! Rick founded Telemachus, whose mission is "Building a community of emerging and experienced leaders engaged in mentoring relationships and intergenerational friendships." The vision is for "vibrant generations of leaders who flourish in serving others." Rick wrote excellent articles on mentoring and hosted an annual retreat for mentors and mentees.

> GOOD MENTORS ASK ABOUT MORE THAN JUST WORK ISSUES.

Rick taught us that good mentors ask about more than just work issues. They know the importance of understanding how things are going with a mentee's family, spiritual life, and health. Without understanding the current dynamics in these areas, a mentor could give good work-related advice that could harm other important life dimensions, such as time with family. (See endnotes for a list of resources by Rick Woolworth.)[40]

Another outstanding mentor-mentee community is Praxis Labs.[41] Praxis has separate Accelerators (in-person training for cohorts) for nonprofit and for-profit Christian social entrepreneurs. Some Praxis Accelerator conferences consist of the CEOs/EDs of twelve social enterprises receiving advice from eight mentors. Chris has been a mentor for each of the last ten years when Nonprofit Accelerators have taken place. They are powerful! Praxis is a great community. It has a transformational vision for redemptive entrepreneurship, as discussed in the foreword to this book by Praxis CEO and cofounder Dave Blanchard. Gaining admission to a Praxis Accelerator is competitive. Participating will likely add great value to your enterprise as well as lifelong friendships with highly talented Christian social entrepreneurs.

You would do well to read other articles on mentoring. Diana Shi wrote "6 Ways to Get the Most Out of the New Mentor-Mentee Relationship."[42] Read her article for different ideas on mentoring.

Being an excellent mentee to outstanding mentors will cause your efforts to bear much more fruit as well as enrich your personal life. You will be well-equipped to pay it back by mentoring others as you go along. Hopefully, you will find mentoring to be as great a joy as we do. We also find that we learn much through our mentoring activities.

Outstanding mentors can change your life. Diligently search for them, prepare for them, and follow up on meetings with them. We encourage you to join formal mentoring communities such as Praxis Labs and Ardent Mentoring, both of which have been created specifically to help you find the very best A+ mentors just when you need them, and to build out these lifelong skills of being a great mentee. As you will see in the next chapter, good mentors can save the day when you enter a crisis.

12

MANAGING THROUGH A CRISIS

AS A CEO/ED you will be confronted with a crisis, and likely several. A crisis can be devastating, but it also can open doors to scale more rapidly. Some say the Chinese word for "crisis" is the same word for "opportunity." In fact, remarkable inventions and great works of music were produced during wars and other catastrophic disruptions in centuries past.

I (Chris) have seen and experienced surprising growth resulting from a crisis. For example, at Edify, our work in Latin America and Uganda dramatically expanded during the pandemic of 2020-22. Two entrepreneurial, innovative managers, one in each of those regions, quickly realized that school entrepreneurs who had not been interested in training online before the pandemic were now enthusiastic about online learning and hearing of solutions that could keep their schools operating remotely. As a result, Edify's work with schools impacted almost twice as many children in 2021 than in the year before the pandemic. I was astonished. I thought the number of children impacted in 2021 would significantly decline. Once again, I realized never to underestimate entrepreneurs!

Crises can occur when you least expect them. Many social enterprises barely avoid going under three or four different times during their existence. It may be any of

> MANY SOCIAL ENTERPRISES BARELY AVOID GOING UNDER THREE OR FOUR DIFFERENT TIMES DURING THEIR EXISTENCE.

dozens of existential threats. Here's a short list you might print off and keep handy to help you see why preparing now for a crisis is important. As a leader you may experience:

FINANCIAL

- Running out of cash
- Big drop in donations/other revenues
- Embezzlement
- Unexpected major expenses
- A recession or depression severely reduces donor giving and your annual cash flow
- Widespread runs on banks in one or more of your countries of operation

GOVERNMENT

- Laws are passed that make what you do illegal or extremely difficult
- An attorney general seeking political gain decides to prosecute your organization
- You or senior staff members are arrested and charged with a crime
- The government announces that it is investigating your organization
- Government raids your offices because your work is revealing corruption or incompetence by the government

GEOPOLITICAL

- War between nations
- Civil war
- Revolution
- Terrorist activities
- Riots

- Coup d'état
- Assassinations

PANDEMIC

- Regional in some or all your areas of operation
- Global
- Supply chain disruptions
- Staff die or become seriously ill for a long time from a pandemic

NATURAL DISASTERS

- Hurricanes, floods, droughts, famines, or fires

INFORMATION TECHNOLOGY

- Your systems are hacked
- Major IT failure and systems not restored for a long period of time
- Major cost overruns and delays on important, new IT initiatives

STAFF

- Death, incapacity, or other loss of several key staff members
- Numerous staff members unite against you or seek to sabotage your organization
- A few disgruntled employees spread damaging lies to the press, your board of directors, or donors
- Staff members play politics, which results in an unmanageable organization unless major personnel changes are made
- Staff member(s) murdered, maimed, or kidnapped in developing countries accompanied by a ransom demand
- Key executives leave to start a competing organization and solicit your donors for donations
- Staff member(s) commit fraud or make major mistakes
- Staff members spread false and damaging rumors

BOARD

- One or more board members decide you should be censured or removed
- Chairperson views self as CEO/ED and does not allow you to do your job
- Board, key executives, major donors, or major partners question your competence or integrity
- Many board members resign in a short period of time

MORAL/ETHICAL/LEGAL FAILURE

- You have an affair or do another immoral act
- You act unethically
- You commit a crime
- You let bad behavior among staff fester so long that organizational culture becomes toxic

LAWSUITS

- You or your organization is sued for injunctions or a massive amount of money, and much of your budget, time, and emotional energy must be devoted to the lawsuit

NEGATIVE PUBLICITY

- Local or national press publishes negative stories about you or your organization

YOUR HEALTH AND FAMILY

- You suffer a debilitating illness or injury
- You suffer burnout
- You neglect family, which results in your being distracted for years trying to repair the damage, or you must resign to give all your attention to rebuilding family relationships

- You neglect your spiritual life and do not seek the Lord in making important decisions, which results in you and your organization suffering significantly from bad decisions

COMPETITION

- Another organization develops a disruptive innovation that is far more efficient, which renders your work obsolete
- Competitors steal a high percentage of your best employees

ENEMIES/CRIMINAL ACTIVITY

- Entrenched interests oppose your programs because they interfere with their profits or progress
- People do not accept you because of your skin color or country of origin and do much to hinder you
- Your offices are flooded or burglarized, and key records and computers are stolen
- Looters ransack your offices and set them on fire or otherwise leave them uninhabitable

YOU

- You make a disastrous decision as a result of not doing careful analysis and getting advice or having had one or more recent big success(es) causing you to be on a "success high" resulting in arrogantly making decisions that go badly
- You do a deal entangling you in financial, legal, reputation, and other problems, which requires massive time and attention away from your core mission
- You continue to run your company after you are too old, or the organization outgrows your competency level

TOTALLY UNEXPECTED BLACK SWAN EVENT

- An astonishing, unprecedented, overwhelming event anticipated by virtually no one is a black swan event. These happen rarely, but they will happen once or twice during your career

We have been through, or helped others through, many of the crises mentioned above. Unfortunately, there are other crises we do not have space to mention here.

The Bible tells us to prepare in advance for crises, and you can survive them with God's help:

> *"The prudent see danger and take refuge, but the simple keep going and pay the penalty." (Prov. 27:12)*

Use the below ideas to help yourself when facing a crisis:

- Have a crisis mentor on speed dial, someone who has successfully navigated multiple crises, whom you can immediately call.
- Conduct an enterprise risk management (ERM) exercise on possible crises, warning signs, and steps you can take. See Chapter 14.
- Identify a PR firm expert who specializes in helping organizations going through a crisis.

Preparing ahead of time can make the difference between your organization going under or surviving. Also, will your organization flourish by taking advantage of opportunities that crises create?

WHEN A CRISIS STRIKES

Along the same line of the prudent leader anticipating danger and taking refuge, we want to help you prepare for a crisis before it happens.

You cannot prepare for every possible issue, but you can have a plan to respond:

Get the facts as best you can. Remember, the first report from the field is almost always wrong. Press in to get multiple confirmations of what you are hearing, as you are likely to be told different information. If there are legal ramifications to the crisis, immediately get the advice of an attorney experienced in crisis management or liability mitigation. In this case, you likely should not make any oral or written statements without the attorney's review and approval. Appoint one person (often it will be you) to be the only one who makes any verbal or written public statements. Tell all others *not* to make *any* statements or answer *any* questions from reporters, as it will be confusing and possibly damaging if numerous executives make comments, some of which will likely be contradictory. Tell everyone, including board members, to refer *all* questions to the one person you appointed. Comments made early in a crisis can come back to haunt you later. Often, saying as little as possible is best, especially before you have gotten advice from attorneys and others who have been through many crises.

> THE FIRST REPORT FROM THE FIELD IS ALMOST ALWAYS WRONG.

Determine who needs to know. Figure out who specifically needs to know of the crisis and the details relating to the crisis, and who does not need to know.

Promptly inform your board chair. Meet with the chair of the board governance committee and any board committee chairs whose area is affected, and ask for their advice and prayers.

Determine a concise statement. Come up with something you can say that is honest, including any qualifiers such as: "We have only a partial understanding; we are diligently attempting to get the facts, and we may have a different understanding once more facts are received." If giving an interview, speak *only* on the talking points upon which you and your advisors have agreed, and nothing else.

Form a crisis management group. This group should consist of board members, key management, outside experts, attorneys with relevant experience, and one or more of your mentors to meet regularly and give you their best advice. With the team's input, develop an ERM scenario exclusively for this crisis. If you do not have a general ERM strategy already in place, develop an ERM now, rather than when in crisis. (Please see the ERM heat map in Chapter 14: Avoiding Pitfalls.)[43]

Form a second team. This second team should consist of street-smart, crisis-experienced advisors who have made hard decisions in crises before. Some should be former or current CEOs/EDs. These three or four advisors will be in addition to your board of directors, and they will meet with you separately. They will advise you on dealing with your board and staff in addition to managing the crisis.

LOOK FOR OPPORTUNITIES TO FLOURISH DURING A CRISIS

Pray and trust in the Lord. When Chris was CEO and majority owner of Comps InfoSystems, he and a board member prayed for the company together every Monday morning for thirty minutes in person for eight years. They prayed for God's guidance to be faithful leaders, to care well for employees, to serve customers well, to make good decisions, and for protection of the company from lawsuits and other harmful attacks. They are convinced the prayers protected the company. Their prayers were particularly helpful when their much larger competitor reduced its prices by half in an attempt to drive Comps InfoSystems out of business. The competing entity made little headway and incurred significant losses for two years. Eventually, Comps acquired it.

There is often a need to reduce expenses to survive a crisis. Here are some approaches to take while in the middle of a crisis:

Conserve cash sooner rather than later. Many organizations implement cash conservation programs too late. So give careful thought to the choice between deep, immediate cost reductions and developing a plan for cost cuts as you gain more information over the next few weeks. Share this and your reasoning behind it with your team.

Now is a good time to let any low performers go. Almost every organization has employees not performing well. Management may be hoping they will turn around in time. However, in a crisis you do not have time to wait. Crisis is a good time to reduce costs by letting go of low performers given the need to conserve cash immediately.

Implement a hiring and wage freeze. Announce to your team that the crisis means that temporarily no new people will be hired, and no salary increases be given.

Do financial projections and plans for your best, realistic, and worst-case scenarios, then create a plan for something even worse than the worst case. Can the organization survive those worse than worst-case ramifications? If not, what else do you need to do right now?

Enforce pay cuts. Ask your highest paid employees and middle managers to voluntarily take the greatest temporary pay cuts they can, ideally 50 percent at the senior level and 30 percent at the middle level. If voluntary cuts do not reach a sufficient level, then implement a uniform pay cut at each of these levels so that average pay of these groups is reduced by 30–40 percent.

Cease all travel unless absolutely necessary. Any travel should require permission of the CEO/ED or COO or CFO.

Determine a particular level of cash decline that will prompt you to furlough x percent of the staff. The first furlough might be 10–33 percent of the staff. When doing furloughs or layoffs, best practice is to furlough more than you think on the first round in hopes that you will not have to do a second round. Organizations that do multiple rounds of furloughs cause much anxiety and uncertainty among staff, prompting some to resign and get jobs elsewhere to avoid being laid off and others to worry or spread rumors. Do not promise that there will be no further layoffs. You can say that you hope the layoff you just did will be the last, but emphasize that nobody knows the future.

Plan for the possible future. Determine how you wish the organization to look if the crisis continues for six to twenty-four months in case revenues/donations decline much more than expected, which will impact your beneficiaries much more than you expect.

> BEING PREPARED TO JUMP INTO ACTION WHEN A CRISIS HITS MEANS YOU WILL BENEFIT FAR MORE PEOPLE YOU SERVE.

Being prepared to jump into action when a crisis hits means you will benefit far more people you serve. An excellent resource to help you with this is from one of the world's top strategy consulting companies. McKinsey & Company has several white papers on crisis management and some that specifically address crisis preparation.[44]

INNOVATING DURING A PANDEMIC LOCKDOWN

As we all now know, regional and global pandemics are real risks. Require your employees to develop new ways to serve clients in a pandemic. Do not allow them to cease serving by thinking nothing can be done. Require them to innovate and implement new solutions.

Edify took this approach when the pandemic caused governments to close all schools in each of the twelve countries of operations. Edify encouraged school entrepreneurs to send teachers into the community to tutor four students at a time, outside and socially distanced, for one hour per day, and then tutor another group of four the next hour, and so on. We learned that one hour of tutoring in a small group can be as valuable as three hours in a classroom.

Another innovation was dropping off homework assignments each day in a central location close to students' homes and simultaneously picking up their previous homework for the teacher to grade. Some teachers texted students Bible verses to meditate on and write about. This improved the students' writing skills as well as discipled them. Some teachers called parents' cell phones to encourage them to ensure their children were spending sufficient time each day on their homework and reading during lockdown. Many schools told us that Edify was the only organization that continued to work with them during the pandemic. They expressed appreciation that Edify shared best practices regarding what other schools were doing to continue educating children during lockdown.

There are many examples in history of innovations during crisis:

- When the Black Plague caused entire populations to stay in their homes, Isaac Newton discovered gravity and calculus. He called his quarantine time the "year of wonders."
- The apostle Paul wrote most of his letters, comprising much of the New Testament, from a prison cell.
- Gideon faced an army of overwhelming numerical superiority, but the Lord showed him an innovative way to rout his enemies (Judg. 7:8).

More recently, we know of a CEO who owned a company who sold locks and other security equipment to locksmiths all over the country. Long before Amazon existed, UPS was the primary large package delivery company. It went on strike, which severely hindered the locksmith entrepreneur and his competitors in delivering their products. So he instructed all his warehouses around the country to rent vans and deliver the locks to customers themselves. He was delivering when his competitors had decided making deliveries was not possible. He increased his market share by 22 percent during this crisis, picking up new customers he had been unable to win over before.

Think diligently on how you can best serve during the crisis through innovation and a can-do attitude. The new ideas you develop will position your organization to serve clients even better after the crisis. Keep these principles in mind during a pandemic:

1. Get the facts, then good advice, and then be decisive.
2. Use lockdown time to strengthen your organization for the future.
3. Seek the Lord's wisdom on decisions during the pandemic.

Numerous futurists predict that another pandemic will occur. An article by McKinsey & Company is worth consulting to inform your preparations for the next pandemic.[45]

In conclusion, crises will befall you. So now is the time to form crisis response teams and develop an ERM heat map with warning alerts and tripwires triggering you to implement response plans. Acting now may well be the difference between surviving or succumbing to the next crisis. Most importantly, regularly pray for your organization for protection against crises and for wisdom and strength to withstand any that occur.

> REGULARLY PRAY FOR YOUR ORGANIZATION FOR PROTECTION AGAINST CRISES.

And be ever mindful of creative opportunities that crises may reveal to serve even better those you seek to transform. Such opportunities may come in the form of partnerships as described in the next chapter. A crisis may open the door to transforming 100x lives if you prepare now to survive, thrive, and capitalize on opportunities that others do not see.

13

PARTNERSHIPS, DEALS, MERGERS, AND ACQUISITIONS

WHILE I (CHRIS) was CEO of Comps InfoSystems, we acquired thirteen other companies. However, one of the first acquisitions failed miserably. A company owner in Phoenix called to say he wanted to sell his company to us because he wished to move to our San Diego headquarters to be near his mother, who was hospitalized close by. He wanted to start working right away at Comps's home office and build a new team. He said we could work out the details of the acquisition over the next few months. The gentleman was a sincere Christian, seemed competent, and appeared to be a good culture fit. His company also would be a good addition to the other products we sold, so I agreed to the deal.

Appearances can be deceiving. Although he was pleasant and sincere, he turned out to be an awful manager. He had 100 percent turnover of his staff in the first few months. He wrote a business plan that made no sense and contained erratic financial projections. Unfortunately, I had not worked out the details of the acquisition because I wanted to wait to see how well his company would work with mine. After four months the situation was clearly untenable. I informed him that we did not wish to buy his company, and he was welcome to take all the remaining employees and assets and continue running his company himself. At that point, he told me that he could not reconstruct his company, so I had to pay him an outlandish purchase price never discussed before.

Had I consulted friends who had done many acquisitions, they would have told me absolutely not to move forward until an agreement was in place. Instead, I had to negotiate a settlement with the gentleman and realize that my settlement money and much time had been needlessly wasted. If I were to do the deal over, I would have structured a purchase price based on performance. That arrangement would have resulted in a minimum payment when he failed.

Experienced dealmakers sometimes speak of how deals are like lobster traps:

They are easy to get into but very difficult to get out of.

Most social entrepreneurs will take part in a partnership, merger, acquisition, or significant transaction once or many times. Well-conceived transactions can thrust your mission forward. Ill-conceived deals and partnerships can hinder you for years or permanently hobble your venture.

In the business world, a well-known fact is that most acquisitions do not work out well. Here are a few of the many reasons for this lack of success:

- Not seeking the Lord's will before beginning negotiations or signing a deal
- Inexperience in doing deals
- Overly optimistic assumptions
- Insufficient care and thoroughness in conducting due diligence
- Lack of culture fit between the two organizations
- Technology integration problems
- Insufficiently researching the other party by getting references from others with whom they have done deals

- Improperly structuring the deal
- Not engaging board members, mentors, legal, accounting, and other advisors highly experienced in doing deals
- Not paying sufficient attention to warning signs that appear
- Paying too much or accepting a price that is too low
- Being too trusting of those on the other side
- Insufficient advance planning for integration of the acquisition or merger into your organization
- The deal was not a good fit with your organization
- Misalignment regarding mission, vision, roles, goals, cultures, worldviews, etc.
- Lack of a clear pathway to financial sustainability or operational success
- Key managers at the acquisition target have no intention of staying

The partnerships, deals, mergers, and acquisitions that do work well are often due to rigorous analysis, very careful planning, and a willingness to abandon negotiations when sufficient indicators show that going forward with the transaction will result in significant problems.

Social entrepreneurs highly capable of running their own operations sometimes charge ahead into dealmaking, where they have little experience—only to fail badly. Say a nonprofit CEO/ED has done an excellent job of managing their organization for many years, and an opportunity arises to purchase a division of another faith-based nonprofit. The division is in the exact same field, the nonprofit has had many interactions with that division, and the CEO/ED knows the management and board well. However, the CEO/ED is inexperienced in making acquisitions. But the CEO/ED might think, *I am in the same field, and I know this organization well. How complicated can it be to acquire the division?* Answer: it can be very complicated, with many pitfalls, if the CEO/ED does not obtain good advice from people highly experienced with partnerships, deals, mergers, and acquisitions.

FIND SEASONED DEALMAKERS

So how can a CEO/ED avoid these pitfalls?

> *Significant problems can be avoided if social entrepreneurs engage one or two of their friends or board members who have bought and sold multiple companies before.*

Without such advice, mistakes are invariably made in the purchase and sale agreement. For instance, not doing due diligence on the condition of the division acquired, not holding the seller accountable for acts done in bad faith during the dealmaking process, and not properly managing the business immediately after the acquisition. These mistakes can cost millions of dollars as well as significant management time and emotional energy.

When making a deal, always consult knowledgeable, trusted advisors about your blind spots. We discuss in Chapter 15 how to use the Johari window in wise decision-making. This will help you define more clearly what is in your blind spot and how you can learn about your blind spots.

In the case of acquiring a division or merging with another nonprofit, social entrepreneur CEOs/EDs often do not identify their blind spots in one or two of the four quadrants of the Johari window: "Do not know what you do not know" and "Think you know but do not." This can have dire consequences regarding documenting complicated acquisitions properly; conducting proper due diligence; negotiating discounts when negative surprises are found during due diligence; integrating an acquisition into your organization; and negotiating not to pay the full price at closing but rather obtaining appropriate holdback provisions to protect against negative, undisclosed problems that might arise six to eighteen months after closing.

Just because the other party is a Christian organization, you should not assume the information you receive from them is accurate. They may innocently provide inaccurate information, or they may be under significant financial pressure and knowingly provide untrue information because they desperately need money. I have seen the latter firsthand.

Many partnerships do not deliver the hoped-for results. The CEOs/EDs of the organizations partnering may see good synergies, but those responsible for making the partnership succeed, often those in middle or lower management, might not wish to make changes, thus the partnership yields little. When a small entrepreneurial organization partners with another company that is large and bureaucratic, the return on investment regarding effort will likely be small. The culture clash often obstructs successful implementation from occurring as well.

Here is some additional advice on making deals:

When partnering with another organization, determine the results you are expecting by certain dates based on certain levels of time and financial commitment. If a return on investment (time, money, results) is disappointing after a reasonable amount of time, withdraw from the partnership after having given the other side sufficient notice that results are less than expected.

> Be sure to build into the partnership agreement clear ways that you can exit the partnership.

Also, have a clause in the agreement that if a significant problem or dispute arises, then you and the CEO/ED or a specified senior executive at the partner organization agree to have two face-to-face meetings—each at least one hour long without lawyers—to solve the problem or dispute. Many problems are quickly resolved when two leaders meet in good faith.

When partnering with another organization, have a provision to exit at any time by making an offer to buy out the other party's interest, such that the other must either accept or choose to buy your interest on the same terms. For example, say a partnership is not going well, and you decide it is worth paying $1 million to buy your partner out. You make an offer to them of $500,000 paid in 30 days, and the other $500,000 paid over three years at 7 percent interest. Your partner must either accept your terms or buy your interest on the same terms. This provision causes each side to be realistic on value. It provides a definitive, time-saving mechanism to move on from a partnership that is not working.

Get references on the other organization. Do they have a reputation for acting in good faith and honoring their commitments? Or did they cause problems for others who did deals with them? I (Chris) was once halfway into doing a major partnership with another organization when I started having checks in my spirit about the other CEO's integrity. I learned that the CEO on the other side of the table had previously done a partnership with a company started by a friend of mine. Upon calling that friend, I learned that the other CEO "does what he thinks is best for his own organization, rather than honor his contractual obligations to a partnership." Thus, I walked away from the deal. A couple of years later, that CEO who did not "honor his contractual obligations" was sentenced to prison for defrauding his shareholders in connection with another deal he did.

Avoid terms that are based on paying a future fair market value. These deals often result in disputes and much time spent in attempting to agree on a fair market value at a future date. Either set a price now for the future, or have a very simple, unambiguous formula to calculate the future price.

When doing a merger, acquisition, or sale of a division or significant assets or rights, engage advisors early with significant experience in such transactions.

Always be ready to walk away from the deal at any time if you see indications that going forward with the transaction will not be very beneficial. Because most deals do not work out, you should be convinced that going forward with the deal will be highly beneficial, even after carefully weighing the risks.

Be sure that you carefully read every word in every agreement that is part of the deal. Do *not* assume your lawyers have carefully protected you in every important area or drafted language that is unambiguous. Even if you engaged the very best lawyers, you will likely find provisions in the agreement to which you object. You do not want to discover those provisions after you sign, but rather before, so you can remedy them.

Do not agree to surprise requests that the other side makes at closing without getting equal or greater concessions in return. Even though both sides have signed a comprehensive contract, some sellers plan on asking for a higher price, and some buyers plan on offering a lower price at the closing or other changes in terms—even though all negotiations supposedly have been resolved by that time. It is up to you either to say no or agree to the surprise request only if the new deal includes equal or sufficiently better terms for your organization.

Last but not least, pray before and during the negotiations. Be sure to follow the four steps in hearing from the Lord as described by Terry Looper and Kris Bearss in *Sacred Pace*, a book we will discuss in Chapter 15.[46] Cancel the deal at any time if you sense the Lord directing you to do so, even if you are led to walk away just before or even at the scheduled closing. As uncomfortable as walking away from a deal may be, doing a bad deal is one hundred times worse. Please keep in mind that "many deals die a death or two" (when the deal is called off), only to be revived later and done with better terms. Walking away may result in a much better deal for you and your organization. Sincerely wait upon the Lord for His divine guidance.

In conclusion, seek the wisdom of many counselors when you are doing deals. Especially have one of your board members who is highly experienced at doing deals be your lead director who will be with you every step of the process, which includes meeting with the other side. Your other board members will look to the lead director for a red or green light to see if the board of directors should approve the deal. Be ever mindful that most partnership mergers and acquisitions do not work out well. Therefore, prepare carefully, spend much time doing due diligence, and always be open to walking away if you or your advisors see indications of significant problems. If you go forward with a partnership, have provisions in the partnership agreement that allow you to exit relatively easily. Most importantly, spend time with your advisors and the Lord in seeking wisdom, which brings us to the next chapter on avoiding costly pitfalls.

14

AVOIDING PITFALLS

MAKING THE MOST of opportunities is important for scaling. Just as important is avoiding pitfalls. Some mistakes can set organizations back years. Other mistakes can cause an organization to fail or the board to decide to change the CEO/ED. Therefore, carefully analyzing threats and risks (both those you have some control over and those you do not) is a critical task for any social entrepreneur. This analysis is an integral part of any good strategic plan. Below are numerous tools to help you identify potential pitfalls.

SWOT Analysis. The CEO/ED and senior management team list the organization's strengths, weaknesses, opportunities, and threats. Make diligent efforts to identify weaknesses and threats, and how to minimize or protect against them. Ask your board and mentors to comment on the SWOT because it is such an important analysis to inform your strategic plan. At Edify, SWOT analysis identified new opportunities, weaknesses needing mitigation or overcoming, and threats to address.

Scenario Analysis. List numerous events that could happen in the next five years that you have no control over. Then rank those events in terms of most likely to happen and most detrimental to your organization. Then list the several that have the highest combined score on a scale of one to ten of most detrimental and most likely to occur. The ones that would be highly detrimental and have a reasonably high chance of occurring are the ones to consider most carefully. Are there steps you can take now to mitigate the risks of them affecting your organization or mitigate the detriment? Are there contingency plans you can develop that can be implemented when you see indications that the detrimental scenarios may be imminent or starting to occur?

Enterprise Risk Management Heat Map. This is a particularly helpful visual for management and your board of directors to understand and analyze risks. Please see below a sample ERM heat map developed by Edify's senior management team in September 2019. On the heat map graph, you plot many risks, both ones you have some control over happening and ones over which you have no control, as discussed in the scenario-planning analysis above. The lower left quadrant contains risks that are not significant and not likely to happen. The graph then expands to the upper left and lower right quadrants that are riskier, until finally reaching the upper right quadrant containing the greatest risks.

Avoiding Pitfalls

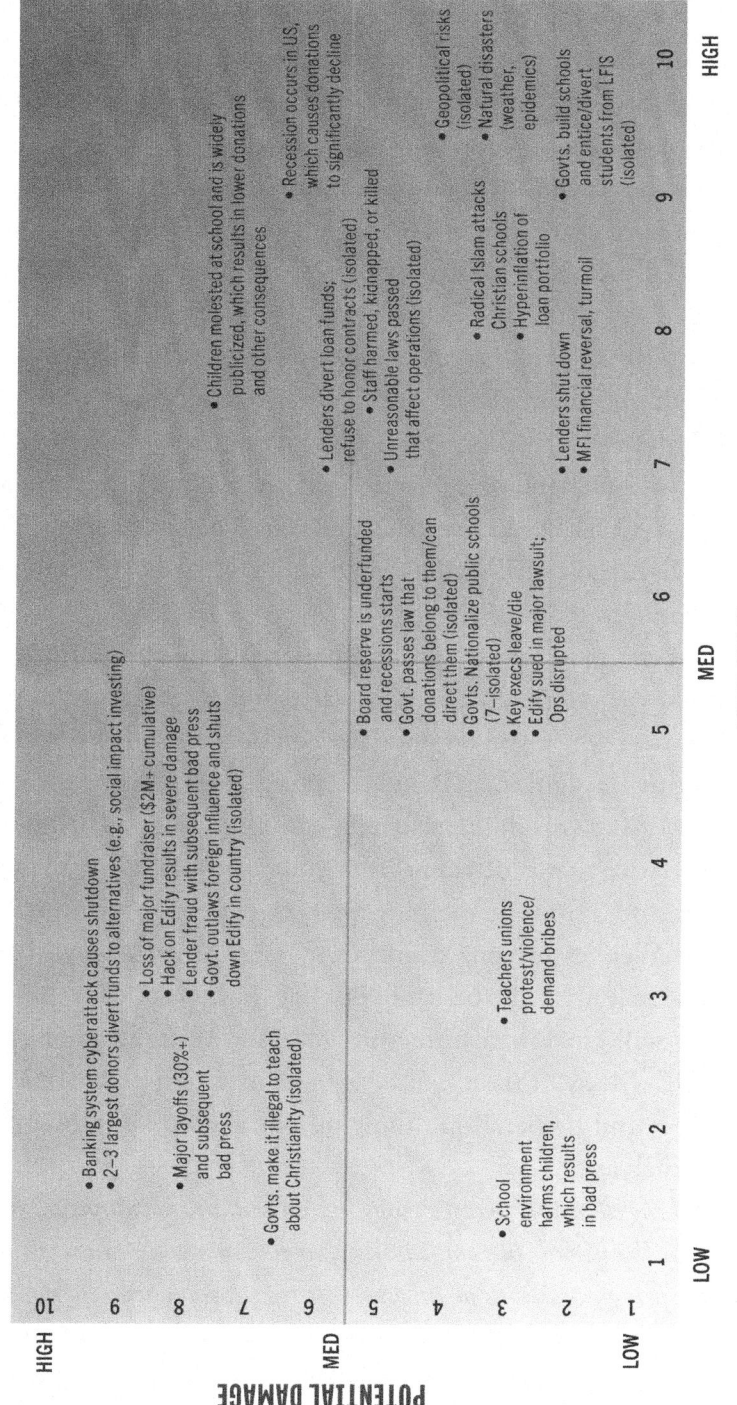

To best inform your thinking when developing the ERM heat map, you would do well to conduct a formal enterprise risk management process. A good guide to this is by McKinsey & Company, a global consulting firm, which wrote the article "A Board Perspective on Enterprise Risk Management."[47] This article simplifies and clarifies the important process of enterprise risk management planning. (Also, Edify's formal ERM process can be found in the endnotes and on *The Social Entrepreneur* portal.)[48]

ERM is an important responsibility for all boards of directors. Although the board chair decides the agenda for board meetings, the CEO/ED often suggests the agenda items by submitting a draft agenda to the chair for approval. A good chairman often adds items that the CEO/ED has not considered or suggested. Ensure that you have a discussion of ERM and update it on the board agenda at least once annually.

Getting good advice whenever making an important decision is always key to your success. Especially obtain good advice when you enter an area where you do not have experience, such as buying a building, taking on significant debt, accepting government funding (which so often comes with hidden strings leading to mission drift), starting a new initiative that is different from your core business, purchasing significant assets from or merging with another organization, etc. Welcome challenges to your thinking by board members with expertise who sincerely wish the best for your organization.

You will encounter numerous risks of falling headlong into other pitfalls. Many of these can be avoided through good advice, careful planning, and preparation. These pitfalls can come in many different forms, such as:

Making decisions that seem optimal to you and your management team, and even the board, but not taking that decision to the Lord in prayer.

Accepting donations or investments from people who do not share your values and who may later attempt to cause you to drift from your mission. Numerous social enterprises that started out helping people living in poverty while also sharing the good news of Jesus eventually devolved into only helping people with little Christian witness other than that many of the staff and board members believe in Jesus. The president of an American Christian college once told Chris that Christian colleges and ministries devolving into secularism is the norm, and those that stay true to proclaiming Jesus are the exception.

When making important decisions, not asking your senior management team, board members with relevant expertise, and wise outside advisors who care about your mission to scrutinize how the decision could be wrong and challenge your intended course of action. This important step in making big decisions well is often not pleasant but is almost always valuable. Chris was CEO of an organization where he and the entire senior management team were convinced that investing many millions of dollars in a new service for disadvantaged people in Africa would greatly benefit them for many years. This turned out to be wrong. Although it did provide some benefit to clients, the expense of the program far exceeded expectations and almost caused the organization to go under. The social enterprise should have done a couple of low-cost probes to see if a successful model could be accomplished. If most or everybody on the management team and the board of directors is excited about an idea, find someone knowledgeable in the field who will aggressively challenge you on how the initiative might fail, or how it could be tested with much less investment of money and time.

Appointing board members who are not passionate about your primary mission. This opens the door to eventual mission drift.

Not carefully hiring for every position in your organization. When two or three people are not passionate about your mission, not competent, or have a negative attitude, they can hurt your culture and even poison the well. Remove them before more damage is done. Hire only A-players as discussed in Chapter 6: Building a World-Class Team on Startup Funding.

Not having an ERM plan that identifies the most significant risks you face. Also, not developing a plan ahead of time to deal with those risks coupled with early indicators and "tripwires" that the risk may soon become a reality.

Not carefully planning. Like the old saying goes, "The person who plans, plans for success."

Pursuing too many initiatives. You will come up with many ideas, and donors and others will suggest many other interesting initiatives to pursue. Sometimes I would go on a trip to the field and come back with several new "great ideas." But my COO had not yet had time to implement many of the "great ideas" from my prior trips. Be careful to avoid overloading your staff with too many "great ideas" that use up valuable bandwidth.

When Chris ran his company, many "great ideas" bounced around in senior management team meetings. Those executives came up with some of the ideas, and salespeople came up with other ideas, and customers came up with still more ideas.

> *Finally, Chris made a list of all the ideas that the executive team thought should be considered. This resulted in sixty-three "great ideas."*

In no way could all these ideas be implemented.

To get the best thinking from trusted executives, each executive ranked each idea on a scale of one to five. An assistant then processed all the rankings and showed them to Chris, identifying the score each executive gave to each idea. Informed by their opinions, Chris reduced the list to the five highest-rated initiatives, in descending order of priority, and then pursued those. He encouraged executives to continue to submit great ideas, but if the new idea was not clearly better than one of the original top five, it would not be pursued until it was deemed better than one of the then current best five ideas. This saved a lot of time and produced greater clarity.

Using your available time to focus on a few very important initiatives is best. Too many meetings consist of interesting brainstorming but result in few actions taken. When an excellent idea comes up in a meeting, ask, "Who has the bandwidth to champion the idea, and when will they accomplish certain milestones?"

Too many unproductive meetings. As alluded to immediately above, it is possible to waste much time on unproductive meetings. These can frustrate your staff and result in fewer people being served. Learn how to hold highly effective meetings, both face-to-face and virtual, for your organization. *Harvard Business Review* and McKinsey & Company have numerous good resources for conducting good meetings.[49]

Not using multiple frameworks for analysis when doing your homework on important decisions. Please consult Chapter 15 on wise decision-making, which speaks of numerous frameworks, such as pros and cons, decision trees, enterprise risk management, risk preference curve analysis, quadrant analysis, ROI in terms of time and money, and weighting/rating templates when recruiting staff or choosing between alternative solutions. Using several of these analyses is helpful to do good homework before taking your decision to the Lord for His divine guidance. The Lord has given us good minds. We should use our minds in preparing for our time with the Lord and requesting His wisdom.

Not thinking through the ROI on an initiative. Why does this opportunity offer such a high return that it merits a financial investment and staff time above other initiatives?

Not scheduling your time. Spend the great majority of your time every day on the most important things you can be doing.

Forgetting to spend a high percentage of your time doing things you enjoy.

Terry Looper is one of the most successful entrepreneurs we know. He works only forty hours per week and has done so since starting his company about thirty years ago.

Terry believes that God directed him to do this after he burned out at a prior company. He says that if he can spend 80 percent of his time on things he enjoys doing, he is at optimum efficiency. Terry goes on to say that if he spends only 75 percent of his time doing work he enjoys, his efficiency drops by 10 percent. If he works only 70 percent on enjoyable tasks, his efficiency drops by 20 percent. (Notice how his efficiency drops twice as much as compared to the decrease in time spent on work he enjoys.)

Terry speaks of 80 percent because almost every CEO/ED has to spend 20 percent of their time doing work they do not enjoy but only they can do. Bill Marriott, then the CEO of Marriott Hotels, once said that if someone else in his organization could do something 70 percent as well as he could, he would delegate that task so he could spend 100 percent of his time on work that required the CEO.[50]

Not having an accountability group who will help you avoid moral failure, ethical lapses, and criminal acts that are sometimes committed inadvertently.

Not encouraging your staff to have a vibrant spiritual life with the Lord so they avoid moral failure or doing something illegal or unethical.

Getting hung up on a "success high." Your organization is growing rapidly and/or getting excellent publicity, you have successfully made a string of important decisions well, donations/revenue are exceeding expectations, you are winning awards, and/or you are hobnobbing with famous people.

Even just one of these success momentums can intoxicate social entrepreneurs into making bad decisions, doing bad deals, focusing less on operations and more on good press and awards, not seeking advice from trusted advisors who will candidly give them constructive criticism, and worst, not humbly and sincerely seeking the Lord. As Solomon warns, "Pride goes before destruction, a haughty spirit before a fall" (Prov. 16:18). An old saying goes, "For every ten people who can withstand failure, only one can withstand success." Significant success will tempt you to think that you need accountability less. The opposite is true. Numerous social entrepreneurs suffered spectacular failures by becoming full of themselves and pushing Jesus away. When things are going great, this is the time to become especially humble, spend more alone time with the Lord, and surround yourself with people who will speak the truth to you.

Chris has a friend whose company grew very rapidly through many successful deals. He then did the biggest deal of all, which blew up. The stock of his publicly traded company plummeted. He lost the great majority of his net worth. The failure made all the major business newspapers and magazines. He said he did not do his normal rigorous due diligence research and did not adequately consider the downsides. He acknowledged the failure humbly and would later give a speech to business groups titled "Pratfall in Center Court."

Giving up. Suppose your organization is doing poorly, you're being criticized often, you have made a string of decisions that appear wrong, you are being falsely accused of wrongdoing, staff are resigning, donations are seriously declining, you are in danger of running out of cash, or you have doubts that God ever called you to do this work. Several of these instances occurring over a prolonged period have caused many entrepreneurs and CEOs/EDs to quit.

Unless you are hearing clearly from the Lord that He wishes you to go somewhere else, please persevere. Although the Lord could possibly be calling you to quit, remember that almost every successful social enterprise experiences converging severe problems like this several times. Sincerely seek the Lord on how He might lead you to make changes and continue serving those God intends you to serve even in the most terrible situations. As Jesus said, "With man this is impossible, but with God all things are possible" (Matt. 19:26). The Scriptures also say:

> *"Trust in the LORD with all your heart, and lean not on your own understanding." (Prov. 3:5)*

We discussed numerous methods to identify risks in this chapter. As helpful as you may find these, much more importance should be given to spending time in prayer and listening to the Lord regarding risks that you might not have identified or might have underemphasized. These are risks that experts might not identify or believe could pose big problems. For example, when Edify's senior management brainstormed future risks in 2018, "pandemic" was put on the list. However, our only prior experience with a pandemic was the Ebola outbreak in four West African countries. Thus, we assumed a pandemic would only be regional and not global. Had we spent more time in prayer, the Lord may have led us to prepare for a global pandemic and to develop plans to continue educating children in lockdown environments in all eleven of our then countries of operations.

If you use best practices for analyzing various alternatives, diligently engage and challenge your own thinking, invite people who care about your mission and are highly experienced in the matter at hand, and earnestly seek the Lord's guidance, you are likely to make the most of good opportunities and avoid seemingly attractive opportunities that will result in harmful pitfalls. This is a path to the wise decision-making discussed in the next chapter.

15

WISE DECISION-MAKING

THERE IS AN old joke: A young business executive says to an older business executive, "How is it that you always make good decisions?"

The seasoned executive replies, "By making many bad decisions when I was younger."

Making wise decisions and implementing them well is almost always the difference between succeeding and failing. You will make bad decisions—every executive does. We hope to help you minimize those bad decisions, especially the major ones, by recommending some proven methods for making wise decisions. First and foremost, do your homework, take your thinking to the Lord for His divine guidance, and then do what He tells you.

So where's a good place to start doing your homework?

PROS AND CONS

Benjamin Franklin is often credited with developing this method of taking a blank piece of paper, making a vertical line separating the two sides of the page, and then listing the positive reasons for a particular decision on one side of the page and the negatives on the other side. Although they have been around for a long time and almost everybody uses them, pros and cons lists are an excellent starting point.

Sometimes the cons are so overwhelming that a compelling case is made not to make the decision. In this case, you should obtain advice from other people regarding the pros and cons that they see, and then take the decision to the Lord in prayer. Be sure to seek the Lord earnestly so you desire His will more than your own as you listen for His answer. If that prayer time gives you a peace about not pursuing this decision, you have saved time and avoided a bad decision.

JOHARI WINDOW

We all have personal biases, hidden assumptions, and blind spots. Seek to identify these, and rid yourself of them so they do not mislead you when using any decision-making tools and when you pray. Ask your executives, board, and mentors to be candid in sharing with you your blind spots because they likely have identified some but may not have voiced them. Analyze past bad decisions for sources of blind spots. Spouses are often excellent at showing us blind spots. Another old joke says, "A person can be a fool their entire life and unaware of it, but not if they are married."

> ASK YOUR EXECUTIVES, BOARD, AND MENTORS TO BE CANDID IN SHARING WITH YOU YOUR BLIND SPOTS.

A useful tool for identifying blind spots is the Johari window. The Johari window is a technique designed to help people better understand their relationship with themselves and others. "It was created by psychologists Joseph Luft . . . and Harrington Ingham . . . in 1955, and is used primarily in self-help groups and corporate settings as a heuristic exercise."[51]

Consulting others regarding areas you don't know can reduce your blind spots and also encourage you to reduce your façade. For social enterprise purposes, a modified version of the Johari window appears below.

KNOWLEDGE OF YOUR FIELD

	WHAT YOU KNOW	WHAT YOU DON'T KNOW
WHAT EXPERTS KNOW	COMMON KNOWLEDGE & BEST PRACTICES	**YOUR BLIND SPOTS** • You don't know what you don't know. • You think you know but your knowledge is false or incomplete
WHAT EXPERTS DON'T KNOW	YOUR UNIQUE KNOWLEDGE & INNOVATIONS	**UNDISCOVERED** • Not yet known • Experts' misconceptions

The left half of the matrix represents information that you know. The right side of the matrix signifies available information that, if known, will lead you to a wiser decision. The upper right quadrant also includes thinking you know certain facts, but in reality, those "facts" are false. A mentor, board member, or colleague who excels at challenging your thinking may uncover some of these. Also, a subject expert on the issue at hand can quickly see what you do not know as well as identify any false information. Proverbs 15:22 says, "Plans fail for lack of counsel, but with many advisers they succeed." Earnestly look for your blind spots by using the resources above. Without identifying blind spots, you may continually make the same bad decisions in the future.

At Edify we seek to increase what is known and decrease what is not. Executives capture what has been learned from operations. For example, when Edify considers bringing the Edify school loan program into a new country of operations, our "new country entry criteria" list, which currently contains seventy-six items, is consulted. And every time Edify researches a new country, the criteria for the list grow because new information is discovered that previously was unknown.

RISK-TO-REWARD RATIO

What is the upside and downside of a particular decision? Always consider the risk-to-reward ratio of every major decision.

It is unfortunately common for entrepreneurs to make decisions with much less upside than downside.

They see an opportunity that looks good and pursue it before thinking through possible negative ramifications. Perhaps they made a similar decision in the past that worked out well but do not consider how circumstances are now different.

Carefully think through what could go wrong, and then put a numerical value on how things going wrong could negatively impact your organization. Then think of what could go right and put a numerical value on how things going well could positively impact your organization as well as a numerical value of the probability of these issues occurring. This relatively fast and easy tool helps avoid bad decisions. It will also highlight some risks that could be mitigated if you go forward.

An example is a nonprofit leader I know who started a major new initiative, thinking it would result in benefiting 30 percent more people. However, the leader was focused on the upside and did not carefully consider that cost overruns could result in 50 percent fewer people being benefited due to the new initiative requiring far greater funding than expected. This resulted in money being taken away from existing successful programs. The new initiative also took away a great deal of management time as it got bogged down with unanticipated problems for several years.

DECISION TREE

The decision tree is a great tool to help you think through complicated decisions that could result in numerous outcomes. (See endnotes for a link to a sample decision tree article.)[52] Chris has found this tool invaluable since he first learned of it in his MBA studies in 1974.

Start with a square on the left side of your page, and then draw several branches from that square listing the possible decisions, with a few branches from each of those potential decisions having possible outcomes. Then estimate a probability of that outcome happening at each of those subsidiary branches. You may have lesser branches extending from each of the subsidiary branches with percentage probabilities assigned to each outcome.

If a good decision tree had been used with the anecdote three paragraphs above, the nonprofit leader would have seen that there was a significant probability of serving 50 percent more people by *not* doing the new initiative. Hopefully, the decision tree analysis would have led to forgoing the risky, calamitous decision that was made. The section below elaborates on decision trees.

RISK PREFERENCE CURVE

The decision tree is an excellent framework for analysis to determine the expected value of various decisions. However, it does not take into account the risk tolerance/appetite of the decision maker. In other words, if a social entrepreneur were presented an opportunity to invest $10,000 in an initiative that was 70 percent likely to return $20,000 and 30 percent likely to return zero, many would simply play the odds and make the investment. With a small investment, your risk aversion is likely low. But if the investment required all the assets of the enterprise, many entrepreneurs would prefer not to take a 30 percent risk of losing everything even though they had a 70 percent probability of doubling the assets. The incremental value of doubling the assets is far less for most entrepreneurs than the loss of losing everything. Thus, risk aversion for a "bet the farm" level of investment may be very high, even though the odds are in their favor.

Sometimes risking everything can result in tremendous results. If the Lord leads you to do so, then obey. When this is not the case, the social entrepreneur would do well to determine the organization's risk appetite through analysis, prayer, and having a sense of how much of the "risk budget" is being consumed by current initiatives at the time the decision will be implemented. If several large, high-risk projects are in the works, you might wish to avoid adding another until the results of the existing projects are clear. If you have very little at risk at a particular moment, that might be the time, contingent upon the Lord's leading, to step out and take a big risk that could result in a great return for God's kingdom. (See a sample risk appetite template at thesocialentrepreneur.org/tools for determining the levels of risk your organization is willing to take in various categories such as mission, governance, reputation, regulatory compliance, security, and programs in the field.)

Careful analysis helps you determine the level of risk relative to reward. A personal example was me making the decision to share my faith with employees at the company where I was majority shareholder. There were lots of reasons not to. Employees might be offended, some could file religious discrimination lawsuits (one did), the company's private equity investor might be upset, and some executives might leave.

However, I decided to look for opportunities to share the saving knowledge of Jesus diplomatically and sensitively with numerous employees. Some received!

That eternal return on investment far outweighed the risks, and I felt the Lord led me to take steps to proclaim Jesus as He gave appropriate opportunities. Diligently seeking the Lord reveals the specific course of action you should take.

An excellent *Harvard Business Review* article was written on this subject: "Better Decisions with Preference Theory."[53] This article shows how decision trees work hand-in-hand with risk preference curves. Please study this excellent article and its good illustrations. Applying it will help you avoid major mistakes. Determining the probability of success of initiatives, and then determining your appetite for risks associated with the initiative, will help you avoid making decisions where the risk-to-reward ratio is against you, or if the odds are in your favor but entail risking too many assets.

POINT OF INDIFFERENCE

This is another analysis that can shed light when making decisions. It means determining the point at which you are indifferent between two choices. For example, you may have two applicants for a job, one of whom is better qualified but requires a higher salary. To determine which person makes more sense to hire, you may conclude that you are indifferent if you must pay a salary of $75,000 to the better-qualified person or $50,000 to the lesser-qualified person. Therefore, if the lesser-qualified person is content with $50,000, you will employ that person instead of the better-qualified person who insists on more than $75,000. However, the better qualified person gets the offer if any amount less than $75,000 per year is acceptable.

QUADRANT GRAPHS

These can be very helpful when weighing multiple important priorities. Below is an example:

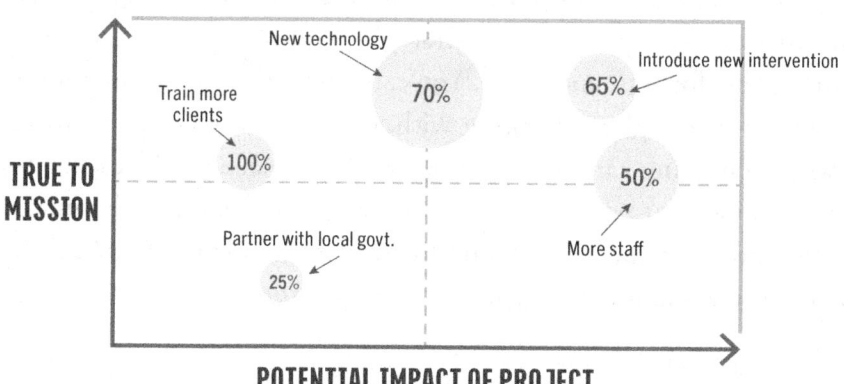

The above graph provides an easy-to-read visual as to initiatives that are mission true as well as highly transformative for those you seek to serve. The size of each bubble represents the amount of investment of money and time required. Thus, an initiative that is in the upper right quadrant that is a small circle indicates a small investment that can have a highly transformative impact in a mission-true manner. This graph provides a dashboard of the opportunities you have identified, and then quickly indicates which provide the greatest impact for advancing your mission most efficiently.

STRATEGIC PLANNING

The strategic plan, in full accord with your mission, is your plumb line to guide you as to which current initiatives you should continue or drop. Embark only on new initiatives that are clearly in accordance with your strategic plan. Social entrepreneurs often love new ideas and fall into the trap of pursuing exciting initiatives not truly in accordance with their strategic plan and mission. An excellent strategic plan with mediocre execution will often yield better results than a mediocre strategic plan with excellent execution.

Many excellent strategic planning models are available. For example, Professor Michael Porter wrote the article "What Is Strategy?" for *Harvard Business Review*, and it is an excellent resource to inform your strategic planning process.[54] This article clarified and simplified strategic planning for Chris.

We encourage you to work with your mentors, board members, and executives most experienced in strategic planning to choose the optimum model for your enterprise. You can also gain much from critiques of your strategic plan. Working with a consultant who specializes in strategic planning can be very helpful. Please make the investment of time and money to develop a good strategic plan that includes metrics to measure your success. Be sure to research trends in your field and obtain ample input from outside experts and those you serve.

It is the CEO/ED's responsibility to develop a strategic plan. The board of directors is responsible for critiquing the strategic plan, requesting changes to it, and when satisfactorily revised, approving the strategic plan.

DISRUPTIVE INNOVATIONS

Be sure your strategic planning process considers how you can develop a disruptive innovation to scale more rapidly with better and cheaper services and products. There are likely disruptive innovations that will result in your impacting far more people than your current approach.

If you search the internet for "disruptive innovations" you'll find numerous examples, such as a mobile banking service allowing users to store and transfer money through their inexpensive, basic mobile phones. M-Pesa was introduced in Kenya as another way for Kenyans, especially disadvantaged people, to have greatly improved access to financial services. Prior to M-Pesa, millions of disadvantaged Kenyans had no access to formal financial services such as banks. Safaricom, the largest mobile phone operator in Kenya, launched M-Pesa in 2007. This service revolutionized making and receiving payments for the poor.[55]

In addition to developing disruptive innovations, be on the lookout for innovations developed by others that you can use to significantly better the lives of those you serve. Microfinance institutions quickly leveraged M-Pesa to collect and distribute loans to their clients and serve people in remote areas that could not be reached cost-efficiently before.

For example, Indeed.com says, "There are many reasons why disruptive innovation can be important. One reason is that it can benefit markets in emerging countries by helping them develop creative solutions that make products [and services] that can be challenging to acquire or use more accessible to their public."[56]

Seek the Lord for these disruptive innovative ideas.

GET INSIGHTS FROM WISE OUTSIDE SOURCES

To help you gain insights from wise outside sources, we encourage you to present your business issues to your mentors or a trusted group of advisors in a systematic way. This could be a personal board of directors or an accountability group that has members with significant life experience.

For example, YPO (formerly Young Presidents Organization) has developed a peer consulting culture whereby organization presidents present their business or personal challenges to seven to twelve of their peer presidents. Over sixty years, this methodology has been proven to work remarkably well. All participants agree to hold everything said during every session in strictest confidence. The member seeking advice often uses the following guidelines when presenting an issue or problem:

1. A concise statement of the issue.
2. What is the goal of the presenter?
3. The background information required to understand the significance of the issue.
4. How does the issue affect the presenter (how do they feel)?
5. What has the presenter tried?
6. What was the outcome as the result of #5?
7. What are the options as the presenter sees them?
8. What does the presenter want and not want from the group?

The meeting begins with a moderator calling the meeting to order. The moderator appoints a scribe before the presentation starts. The scribe will take notes regarding advice given to the presenter so they can focus on the advice instead of attempting to make notes during the session. The moderator asks all in attendance to agree to keep entirely confidential everything said by the presenter and all others during the session. During the first half of the allotted time, the moderator allows only clarifying questions but no advice. After all clarifying questions have been asked and answered, the moderator gives each person the opportunity to share their advice with the presenter.

At the end of the presentation, the presenter tells the group what they heard, shares their feelings on what was said by the group, tells the group whether they fulfilled the presenter's needs, and challenges the group to do more if it didn't fulfill the needs. The moderator asks all who took any notes to give them to the presenter, so the notes are never seen accidentally by someone else. The moderator concludes the meeting by reminding everyone that everything said was strictly confidential and can never be discussed again unless the presenter is present and invites discussion on the issue.

For major decisions, you may wish to hire a professional moderator to obtain the best input from the group.

If you use these guidelines for your presentations, you will gain much better insights from those from whom you seek counsel.

As with all important decisions, consult one or more of your mentors for wisdom. (Please refer to our advice on choosing great mentors in Chapter 11.) Time and again, mentors have been invaluable to Lloyd and Chris in reaching good decisions.

PREPARING FOR WISE DECISIONS

Putting in place early the pieces needed to make wise decisions will greatly improve the likelihood of making excellent choices and 100x impact. These include the following:

- Finding a good set of mentors.
- Developing a personal board of directors. This is different from an organizational board. It is a group of three to five wise people who care much about you and will regularly bring their candid perspective and advice to help you build the life you desire in

addition to the organization's goal. (Consult the endnotes for resources for building a personal board.)[57]
- Appointing a board of directors for your organization with the key skills and passion your organization needs and a wealth of board governance experience.
- Frequently using many or all the decision-making tools described in this chapter.
- Implementing a good strategic plan and ERM plan.
- Hiring wise attorneys, accountants, and other professionals and experts in your field who will serve you well at key decision points, especially when urgent decisions need to be made.
- Maintaining a robust spiritual life that incorporates much prayer.

WISDOM COMES FROM THE LORD

The most important step you can take in making wise decisions is to pray and earnestly seek the Lord's guidance. If it is a particularly big decision, praying and fasting for a day or two or three often yields the greatest clarity on God's direction.

Terry Looper and Kris Bearss authored *Sacred Pace*, which is the best book we have read for making decisions through seeking the Lord and doing pre-decision homework. It is an easy-to-read, enjoyable book. They explain the four-step process Terry has used for decades in building his privately owned company, which he started with limited capital and grew to over $6 billion in sales without ever taking any venture capital or private equity. As mentioned earlier, Terry did this by working only forty hours per week, except in those rare occasions of major pressing issues.

Here are Terry's four steps:[58]

1. Consult your friend Jesus.
2. Gather the facts.
3. Watch for circumstances.
4. Get neutral.

We highly recommend that you read this book and regularly consult it when making decisions. The majority of what we have written in this chapter helps you address Terry's second step ("Gather the facts").

Sometimes social entrepreneurs shortchange themselves by focusing only on the analysis done by themselves and their advisors. Although such analysis is important, the Lord's guidance must be sought to arrive at the best decision. The omniscient Creator of the universe, who loves you dearly, is always ready and delighted to guide you. For your sake and the sake of those you serve, seek the Lord. James 1:5 tells us, "If any of you lacks wisdom, you should ask God, who gives generously to all without finding fault, and it will be given to you."

16

CRANE'S PIVOTAL PRINCIPLES OF SOCIAL ENTREPRENEURSHIP

DURING MY TWENTY years as a social entrepreneur, both failures and successes prompted me (Chris) to develop a list of principles. I believe you would find it helpful to have these in one place. Some of these have not been mentioned earlier in the book, and those that have been mentioned may be expressed somewhat differently here to add perspective.

INDIVIDUAL PRINCIPLES

You will be most effective if genuine care and love motivate you. Truly see yourself as a servant to those you seek to assist. Leave personal ambitions behind. As Pastor Rick Warren says near the beginning of *The Purpose Driven Life*, "It's not about you."[59] It is all about loving God, loving others as you love yourself, and diligently serving them.

Diligently seek the Lord and obey His leading. Examine your motives. Avoid working to gain recognition for yourself or your organization, to win awards, to accomplish something big, or for other selfish ambitions.

Schedule time to pray and fast as you seek the Lord's will for how you serve others. Lloyd has scheduled three silent spiritual retreat days a year for more than twenty years. Habits like these lend themselves to hearing from the Lord. If you are married, be sure to talk and pray with your spouse about major decisions.

Diligently persisting in your work over a long period of time will result in great joy. However, you will also have disappointments. You may be discouraged to the point of quitting several times, and you will likely run out of cash or other resources several times. You will be misunderstood and even mistreated by those you serve, by other organizations, and even by your fellow coworkers. Despite all of this, be determined to stay on the mission that God has given you. If you are true to His mission for you, no matter what happens, you will succeed.

Combine the Great Commission (sharing Jesus and discipling) with the Great Commandment (loving God and others). Beware of too much focus on helping others and too little focus on telling them about Jesus and encouraging them to grow in their faith.

When you truly serve others because of your relationship with God, people are often receptive to hearing how Jesus inspires you.

Speak about Jesus in a culturally sensitive manner at every appropriate opportunity in your community or workplace.

ORGANIZATION PRINCIPLES

Beware of mission creep. Only pursue new initiatives that are truly in accordance with your core mission. Avoid trying to do too many activities. Have outside board members or an external organization such as On Mission review your activities every two or three years to ensure you are staying true to your mission.[60]

People in developing countries may tell you what you want to hear to get your money or keep their jobs. Have an independent way to verify what you are being told. After locals have told you they have deployed funds, do spot checks to make sure all funds were used as agreed.

Do not let donors' agendas take you off course. It is best to decline a donation with requirements not in accordance with your mission.

Conduct careful due diligence. Be sure you know who controls the funds you provide and how they will be used. If you are building a school, a church, an orphanage, a hospital, etc., in whose name will the title to the land vest? Will it be in the name of a properly organized local charity/foundation with good governance or in the personal name of the pastor, missionary, or other national with whom you are dealing? If an individual has the title to the land, they probably have the legal right to sell the land and the buildings you financed at any time and pocket all the proceeds. This happens.

There are highly capable nationals. It may take effort to find a national who will do an excellent job as the head of country operations or in other senior executive roles for your organization in a country. It is worth making this effort because in the long term, nationals should hold the top positions in their country.

Obtain good mentors. You should especially seek out experienced social entrepreneurs who can help you scale more rapidly and solve problems better through godly advice. Attend a program such as Praxis Accelerator to learn how to be a better Christ-centered social entrepreneur. Seek mentoring at Ardent Mentoring (ardentmentoring.org).

Hire and retain only A-players. These are people who:

- Are very good at the tasks the job requires
- Are a strong culture fit
- Are passionate about your mission and work
- Have a great attitude

> SEEK MENTORING AT ARDENT MENTORING (ARDENTMENTORING.ORG).

Develop a strong board of directors. These should be people who understand board governance best practices and bring the skills your enterprise needs. Select your board members very carefully. A misaligned director can cause significant problems. The right director can move your organization forward in wonderful ways. Appoint directors only if they are passionate about your core mission. They must be fully aligned with the mission that God has given you.

PARTNER PRINCIPLES

Make a grant, loan money, or invest your time only with recipients who are diligent and will be held accountable. Some will not use your money for the purposes agreed upon. Others will not provide reports on the use of your money.

Be sure to determine if beneficiaries have the capacity to use funds effectively. If they do not, you risk overloading them with debt.

Make every reasonable effort to be culturally sensitive. Understand that certain practices in your culture may be foreign or even offensive to the people you seek to serve. However, always use certain best practices, even in the face of objections, especially practices concerning the appropriate use of money with those you serve or partner with.

Governments can have different agendas than yours. Sometimes they focus more on looking good than offering real benefits. They can be short-term oriented rather than long-term. They can hinder you. However, a government can be an ally. Keep an open mind to assess potential value through creating partnerships with governments. However, if after significant effort the government is not responsive other than saying they like your program, be prepared to move on without the government.

PROGRAM PRINCIPLES

Do not do for the poor what the poor can do for themselves with reasonable efforts and expense. Give them the dignity in doing what they can, and you assist with what they cannot.

Do no harm. Aid often does more harm than good; it can take away people's incentives to improve themselves and make them dependent rather than self-sustaining. Avoid creating an entitlement mentality among those who can work their way out of poverty with development assistance as opposed to handouts.

Determine the ROI of a proposed intervention. How much lasting change will occur in how many people's lives per hundred dollars invested?

Understand the real needs of the people you seek to serve. Look for tangible evidence that there are unfilled needs that locals wish to be filled. Do not assume that because you, the outsider, see a solution to a problem, it will be welcomed in the region you wish to serve. Consult community leaders and other organizations serving in that community for advice. Pray without ceasing!

Focus your efforts so they are effective and can achieve scale for large impact. Avoid having so many initiatives that none provide benefit.

Seek the Lord regarding how quickly you should grow your program. Numerous organizations try to grow too quickly and encounter problems. Other organizations stay small for too long because of a lack of focus on growing to serve more people.

A theory of change is a theory, not necessarily an action plan. An action plan requires some early experimentation and low-risk/low-cost failures before making bigger investments for larger impacts. Develop the best theory of change you can, and continually revise it based on implementation results.

In many developing countries, a high correlation between dire poverty and corruption exists. If you do not take steps to overcome a culture of corruption, the same debilitating poverty that exists today may continue for decades in the future despite your efforts. Thus, only teaching ethics as part of your work may not be sufficient to cause someone to be honest rather than extorting or paying bribes. But if people believe that God will hold them accountable for their actions, they are more likely to act with integrity. Teach about Jesus and the importance of applying His principles of honesty to overcome corruption, love to overcome hate, unselfishness to overcome greed, peacemaking to overcome violence, and servant leadership to overcome self-serving leadership. Define your model to overcome systemic obstacles to long-lasting change such as corruption and oppression. Only Jesus can overcome these formidable barriers.

> ONLY JESUS CAN OVERCOME THESE FORMIDABLE BARRIERS.

MONITORING, EVALUATION, AND METRICS PRINCIPLES

Measure results in an unbiased manner and with unbiased people doing the measuring. It may be helpful to have a university or other credible entity conduct the evaluations.

Evaluate your interventions to determine their effectiveness. Interventions that are not carefully inspected may be of little value, will likely not achieve full potential, and have little credibility with donors.

Be impact/results-oriented, not input/output-oriented. The issue is not how many people started or finished your program but rather how much their lives were changed for the better. Judge yourself and others on outcomes, not inputs.

Engage a metrics expert to assist you in establishing the right measurements for your work.

Avoid thinking that your work is too difficult to measure. Hope International has seven different metrics to determine spiritual growth among clients, staff, and the entire organization. If showing direct causation of a benefit is difficult, proxy measures can likely show high correlation of benefit from your interventions. Come up with the best metrics you can, as many donors will insist on some metrics. The book *Social Entrepreneurship* by Arthur C. Brooks has an insightful chapter titled "Measuring Social Value."[61] The entire book is excellent with much practical information for social entrepreneurs at any stage of development.

WHERE TO GIVE TO SUPPORT SOCIAL ENTERPRISES

Ask yourself if the social enterprise has good governance and real accountability. Many organizations have complicated structures that are unwieldy. They may use money inefficiently because of excess bureaucracy or dysfunctional or overlapping board structures.

Consider several angles. What is the theory of change/transformation at an organization? Will it bring about real and lasting change? Is there a practical plan to implement the theory of change through experienced people? Will it result in systemic change in the geographical area served?

Determine if the program is sustainable and built to last. When you, your staff, and funding leave the location served, will the program continue or collapse? If it is not financially sustainable, long-term continuation may be low.

Consult local experts. I have found that expats and organizational leaders who are new to a country or culture often think they know more than they actually do, and as a result they neglect to consult local experts or other expats who have years of experience in that setting.

Be sure the CEO/ED of the organization has a good strategy and a strong team to implement that strategy. Does the senior leadership team have a track record of success? Require that the organization be financially transparent and provide reports on its results, not just activities.

HOW TO GIVE TO SUPPORT SOCIAL ENTERPRISES

Be careful not to stipulate activities that are outside the mission of the organization. Chris knows a social enterprise that was founded to share the gospel of Jesus in combination with helping disadvantaged people materially, socially, and economically. However, twenty-five years later, the organization pursued government funding, which stipulated the organization could no longer proselytize. The Great Commission is no longer prioritized. The social entrepreneur, who founded the organization but was no longer active in management, was heartbroken.

If you make significant contributions to a social enterprise, have a contract stipulating that they must achieve certain outcomes or improvements to continue to receive funding. Don't transfer all funds on the front end, but phase in the loans/grants over time based on achieving certain benchmarks.

Specify the reports that you will receive. Make it clear that if you do not receive the reports in a timely manner, your donations will stop.

Whenever possible, inspect what is being done in the field. Do not just speak with the management of the organization; rather, find ways to speak with the beneficiaries without management present.

CONCLUSION: THE WAY FORWARD

AS YOU KNOW, our desire is that this book will be a portal into resources, best practices, and a tribe of smart Christian social entrepreneurs and mentors who can help you. As a result, we want to see an explosive inflection point of growing at a faster rate in your organization's success and impact—100x impact, God willing.

But the only way this book and the surrounding body of resources and mentors will be helpful is if you distill your learning down into written action areas and then follow through. We want to help you make that happen.

First, if you write down your learnings, goals, and action commitments, there is a substantially higher chance they will happen. Just by writing them down, you dramatically increase the chance of success! Our advice is to limit the number of primary action areas to just a handful. We have found that there is a substantially higher chance you will make progress in those areas. Second, share your learning and your plan with friends, peers, and mentors. If you share your plan, not only do you gain insights, but the chances are substantially higher that you will stay focused and follow through on the plan.

We want to make both of those very simple for you to do. To help you, we are asking you to make the following investments:

1. *Create a 100x Social Entrepreneur Road Map.* Take one hour and condense all your learning from this book into a one-page "100x Social Entrepreneur Road Map," which will help you capture your mission, long-term metrics, family vision, action areas around your own life, your leadership, the people around you, and perhaps one

other action point. Don't try to get it perfect. Just invest one hour in the plan, and then begin to share it with your advisors. Send us a copy, and we will, time permitting, give you our reflections and advice as well. (Consult endnotes to download the template.)[62]

2. *Join the Tribe.* This network of peers will provide you deeper tools and resources on these same topics to lift you and your social enterprise to the next level. Go to thesocialentrepreneur.org/tools.

3. *Find a seasoned, godly mentor.* If you are serious about what you learned in this book and want to be matched with a wise mentor, in 2022 we cofounded Ardent Mentoring to connect qualified social entrepreneurs with some of the most successful Christian leaders, whom you might otherwise have no way of meeting. These leaders have a desire to give back and invest time in emerging social entrepreneurs who they believe may produce 100x impact. Visit the Ardent Mentor portal at ardentmentoring.org.

You will greatly increase the probability of succeeding as a social entrepreneur if you do the above.

Also, you will greatly increase your ability to impact the world 30x, 60x, or 100x if you apply the key principles from the three sections of *The Social Entrepreneur:*

- Diligently become a self-disciplined Chief Life Officer, and consistently seek the Lord's guidance (Part 1).
- Follow our steps to becoming a transformational social entrepreneur who builds an outstanding team of employees and board of directors and stays true to mission (Part 2).
- Follow our advice for fundraising effectively, making wise decisions, choosing great mentors to guide you, making smart deals, avoiding pitfalls, and navigating through crises (Part 3).

The two of us have used the principles in this book to impact millions of people. Lloyd has 23,000 hours of advising high-capacity executives and social entrepreneurs to transition to helping others through social enterprises. These competent people have then benefited countless others. Chris's microfinance work impacted 4 million entrepreneurs and approximately 12 million dependents in addition to his work with 12,000 low-fee Christian schools that educate 3 million children in developing nations.

Lloyd has been a social entrepreneur for twenty-five years and Chris for twenty years. You may be sufficiently young that your social entrepreneur journey will last many more years than ours. As a result, you likely will transform far more lives!

ONE LAST THOUGHT

There is a confluence of several important developments now funneling wind into the sails of social entrepreneurs:

- Ever-improving, inexpensive or free communication technology, such as apps, video conferencing, and social media, all being widely used in many of the poorest areas of the world to share ideas, identify best practices, conduct meetings and trainings, mentor, and do banking remotely.
- Bright people ranging from recent college grads to experienced executives and entrepreneurs looking to work at social enterprises that have world-changing visions.
- Christian mentors excited to invest their wisdom in social entrepreneurs.
- Christian venture philanthropists willing to donate or invest in sound social enterprises.

As a result, one person can now impact many millions of people more than in the past.

Perhaps you are one of those people. We want to help you transform the lives of 30x, 60x, or even 100x the number of disadvantaged people who can greatly benefit from your efforts. As a social entrepreneur seeing 100x impact, you will have great adventures, meet amazing people, power through big challenges, and fail sometimes but then regroup and overcome. You will enjoy the profound fulfillment of having jumped all in on efforts that resulted in many lives being transformed!

This work will be daunting at times, but remember what the Lord commanded Joshua: "Be bold and strong! Banish fear and doubt! For remember, the Lord your God is with you wherever you go" (Josh. 1:9, TLB). Take a bold step and connect with Ardent Mentoring, which will take the bold step of seeking the best resources and network of seasoned leaders to meet you when you do.

God bless you for investing your life in loving God, loving others as yourself, and sharing Jesus.

APPENDIX 1

SUGGESTED READING FOR FURTHER STUDY

Social Entrepreneurship: A Modern Approach to Social Value Creation by Arthur C. Brooks

When Helping Hurts: How to Alleviate Poverty Without Hurting the Poor . . . and Yourself by Steve Corbett and Brian Fikkert

The Poor Will Be Glad: Joining the Revolution to Lift the World Out of Poverty by Peter Greer and Phil Smith

Mission Drift: The Unspoken Crisis Facing Leaders, Charities, and Churches by Peter Greer and Chris Horst with Anna Haggard

The Board and the CEO: Seven Practices to Protect Your Organization's Most Important Relationship by Peter Greer and David Weekley

Toxic Charity: How Churches and Charities Hurt Those They Help (And How to Reverse It) by Robert D. Lupton

African Friends and Money Matters: Observations from Africa by David E. Maranz

More Than Good Intentions: Improving the Ways the World's Poor Borrow, Save, Farm, Learn, and Stay Healthy by Dean Karlan and Jacob Appel

A Dream and a Coconut Tree: Transforming Education for the Poor by Christopher A. Crane

Why Startups Fail: A New Roadmap for Entrepreneurial Success by Tom Eisenmann

And most important: the Bible

WEBSITES TO VISIT

Praxis website: praxislabs.org

Ardent Mentoring website: ardentmentoring.org

Telemachus website: telemachusnetwork.org/resources

APPENDIX 2

PHOTOS OF CHRIS CRANE'S SOCIAL ENTREPRENEURSHIP IN THE FIELD

Chris Crane at a low-fee Christian school in Ghana

Jane Crane, wife of Chris, at an Edify partner school in Ghana

Chris Crane with new friends at an Edify partner school in Liberia

NOTES

1. Sarah H. Alvord, L. David Brown, and Christine W. Letts, "Social Entrepreneurship and Societal Transformation: An Exploratory Study," *Journal of Applied Behavioral Science* 40, no. 3 (September 2004): 260–282, doi.org/10.1177/0021886304266847.

2. J. Gregory Dees, "Social Enterprise: Private Initiatives for the Common Good," *Harvard Business Review* 76 (Winter 1998): 54–58.

3. David Martyn Lloyd-Jones, quoted by Tim Keller, "What Is Gospel-Centered Ministry?" The Gospel Coalition National Conference, May 28, 2007, thegospelcoalition.org/conference_media/gospel-centered-ministry/.

4. Dictionary.com, s.v. "entrepreneur (*n.*)," accessed June 20, 2022, dictionary.com/browse/entrepreneur.

5. Jean-Baptiste Say, quoted in "Entrepreneurship," *The Economist*, April 27, 2009, economist.com/news/2009/04/27/entrepreneurship.

6. gallup.com/cliftonstrengths/en/home.aspx.

7. Eugene Peterson, *The Pastor: A Memoir* (Colorado Springs: NavPress, 2002), 239.

8. José Ortega Gasset, *The Revolt of the Masses*, rev. ed. (1930; repr., New York: W.W. Norton & Company, 1994), 104.

9. Johann Wolfgang von Goethe, quoted in Howard Schultz, *Pour Your Heart into It: How Starbucks Built a Company One Cup at a Time* (New York: Hachette Books, 1999), 110.

10. Chris Crane and Tiger Dawson cofounded Edify in 2009 because it was difficult for children living in poverty in Africa and Latin America to obtain a good education. Teachers at public schools are often absent or otherwise not teaching. Although they were supposed

to be free, public schools often charged hidden fees. Those schools were often overcrowded with eighty to one hundred students per classroom. Therefore, many children were not gaining the skills needed to work their way out of poverty and better provide for their families in the future.

In response to this problem, Christians living in disadvantaged communities started schools charging low fees, often fifty cents to one dollar per day per student in 2022 purchasing power. Despite such modest fees, if a school had 250 children or more, it was usually fully financially sustainable. They received no government subsidies whatsoever or donations from anyone. The schools typically started with a kindergarten and added one classroom per year. There was almost always a need to build more classrooms or other infrastructure. Virtually no microfinance institutions were making loans to these Christian schools.

Edify raised donations in the US and loaned those funds to local Christian microfinance lenders, who would then loan the funds to the Christian schools, which would repay through monthly installments over three years. Building an entire classroom typically cost $8,000–$15,000. The lender would charge sufficient interest to cover its cost and make a small profit.

As of March 31, 2022, Edify has partnered through loans and training with approximately 12,000 low-fee, financially sustainable Christian schools educating about 3,258,000 children in seven African nations and five Latin American nations. The training provided by Edify's staff of 110 people, all nationals working in their own countries, includes better academic and Christian education, better school management techniques, and education technology for students. For more information, please go to edify.org.

11. Clayton M. Christensen, "How Will You Measure Your Life?" *Harvard Business Review* (July–August 2010): hbr.org/2010/07/how-will-you-measure-your-life.

12. "Howard Hendricks Tribute," Dallas Theological Seminary, dts.edu/howard-hendricks-tribute/.

13. Dr. Bobby Clinton, quoted in "Bobby's Six Values," Vantage Point3, February 13, 2019, vantagepoint3.org/bobbys-six-values.

14. Christensen, "How Will You Measure Your Life?"

15. Bob Shank, "The Foundation Assessment," The Master's Program, priorityliving.org/tmp/. (Adapted with permission.)

16. Jim Collins, *Great By Choice: Uncertainty, Chaos, and Luck—Why Some Thrive Despite Them All* (New York: Harper Business, 2011), 39–68.

17. Go to the portal (thesocialentrepreneur.org/tools) for a sample potential-hire rating sheet.

18. Go to the portal (thesocialentrepreneur.org/tools) for an interview review template.

19. Go to the portal (thesocialentrepreneur.org/tools) for a new board member onboarding process.

20. Go to the portal (thesocialentrepreneur.org/tools) for a sample board skill map.

21. Go to the portal (thesocialentrepreneur.org/tools) for a sample succession plan.

22. Visit the Ardent Mentoring portal (ardentmentoring.org).

23. Walt Rakowich, interview by Josh King, "Episode 201: Former Prologis CEO Walt Rakowich Is Transparent About Transfluence," October 14, 2020, in *Inside the ICE House*, produced by Kearney Ferguson, podcast, YouTube Video, 59:43, youtube.com/watch?v=krxEqCIptFk.

24. Harvard Business School, Strategic Perspectives in Nonprofit Management (exed.hbs.edu/program-finder?topic=Social%20Enterprise%20%26%20Nonprofits). Tuition in 2023 was $7,000.

25. Harvard Business School programs (exed.hbs.edu/program-finder?topic=Social%20Enterprise%20%26%20Nonprofits).

26. *Stanford Social Innovation Review*, ssir.org.

27. Harvard Social Enterprise Initiative (hbs.edu/socialenterprise/about/).

28. Becca Spradlin (founder, On Mission, onmissionadvisors.com), in discussion with author on July 30, 2021

29. Ibid.

30. Peter Greer and Chris Horst, *Mission Drift: The Unspoken Crisis Facing Leaders, Charities, and Churches* (Bloomington, MN: Bethany House Publishers, 2015), 91–93, 113, 115, 185).

31. "History," ChildFund, accessed August 8, 2022, childfund.org/about-us/history.

32. Wikipedia, s.v. "ChildFund," last modified July 18, 2022, en.wikipedia.org/wiki/ChildFund.

33. Jim Towey, "Mother Teresa and the 'Sisters Who Stay,'" *Wall Street Journal*, September 1, 2022, wsj.com/articles/mother-teresa-and-the-sisters-who-stay-calcutta-charity-missionaries-catholic-soup-kitchen-faith-service-food-distribution-11662046627.

34. Becca Spradlin, discussion with author.

35. Visit thesocialentrepreneur.org/tools to access a sample template.

36. "Ethical Standard 22," *AFP*, accessed August 8, 2022, afpglobal.org/ethicsmain/code-ethical-standards.

37. Go to the portal (thesocialentrepreneur.org/tools) to download a template for assessing fundraisers.

38. Fred Smith Jr., "What to Look for in a Mentor," *The Gathering Blog*, September 21, 2017, thesmithslant.com/would-you-be-my-mentor.

39. Peter Drucker, "5 Essential Questions for Entrepreneurs," *Inc.*, September 5, 2013, inc.com/peter-economy/5-essential-questions-entrepreneurs.html.

40. Visit the portal (thesocialentrepreneur.org/tools) and telemachusnetwork.org to download resources by Rick Woolworth.

41. praxislabs.org.

42. Diana Shi, "6 Ways to Get the Most Out of the New Mentor-Mentee Relationship," *Fast Company*, July 7, 2020, fastcompany.com/90529135/6-ways-to-get-the-most-out-of-a-new-mentor-mentee-relationship.

Notes

43. This McKinsey & Company white paper will inform your thinking on ERM scenarios: André Brodeur et al., "A Board Perspective on Enterprise Risk Management," *McKinsey Working Papers on Risk*, Number 18, February 2010, mckinsey.com/~/media/McKinsey/Business%20Functions/Risk/Our%20Insights/A%20board%20perspective%20on%20enterprise%20risk%20management/A%20board%20perspective%20on%20enterprise%20risk%20management.ashx.

44. Sanjay Kalavar and Mihir Mysore, "Are You Prepared for a Corporate Crisis?" *McKinsey Quarterly*, April 17, 2017, mckinsey.com/business-functions/risk/our-insights/are-you-prepared-for-a-corporate-crisis.

45. Gemma D'Auria and Aaron De Smet, "Leadership in a Crisis: Responding to the Coronavirus Outbreak and Future Challenges," McKinsey & Company, March 16, 2020, mckinsey.com/business-functions/organization/our-insights/leadership-in-a-crisis-responding-to-the-coronavirus-outbreak-and-future-challenges?cid=eml-app.

46. Terry Looper and Kris Bearss, *Sacred Pace: Four Steps to Hearing God and Aligning Yourself with His Will* (Nashville: Thomas Nelson, 2019).

47. Brodeur et al., "A Board Perspective on Enterprise Risk Management."

48. Visit the portal (thesocialentrepreneur.org/tools) to download Edify's formal enterprise risk management process.

49. *Harvard Business Review*, hbr.org/search?search_type=&term=how+to+run+a+meeting&term=); McKinsey & Company, mckinsey.com/search?q=meetings%20successful.

50. Dale Van Atta, "How Bill Marriott Balanced Being a Bishop, Father, and CEO of a Multi-Million Dollar Company," *LDSLiving*, October 12, 2019, ldsliving.com/how-bill-marriott-balanced-being-a-bishop-father-and-ceo-of-a-multi-million-dollar-company/s/91727.

51. Wikipedia, s.v. "Johari window," last modified June 14, 2022, wikipedia.org/wiki/Johari_window.

52. Wikipedia, s.v. "Decision tree," last modified June 6, 2022, en.wikipedia.org/wiki/Decision_tree. See endnote 53 for more information on decision trees and a sample of a decision tree.

53. John S. Hammond III, "Better Decisions with Preference Theory," *Harvard Business Review* (November 1967): hbr.org/1967/11/better-decisions-with-preference-theory.

54. Michael Porter, "What Is Strategy?" *Harvard Business Review* (November–December 1996): https://hbr.org/1996/11/what-is-strategy.

55. safaricom.co.ke/personal/m-pesa.

56. "What Is Disruptive Innovation? Definition, Importance and Examples," Indeed, last modified March 1, 2022, indeed.com/career-advice/career-development/innovation-disruption.

57. Visit the Ardent Mentoring portal (ardentmentoring.org).

58. Terry Looper and Kris Bearss, *Sacred Pace*, xiii.

59. Rick Warren, *The Purpose Driven Life: What on Earth Am I Here For?* (Grand Rapids: Zondervan, 2002), 21.

60. onmissionadvisors.com.

61. Arthur C. Brooks, *Social Entrepreneurship: A Modern Approach to Social Value Creation* (London: Pearson, 2008), 65.

62. Go to the portal (thesocialentrepreneur.org/tools) for a sample road map.

ABOUT THE AUTHORS

CHRISTOPHER A. CRANE acquired Comps InfoSystems in 1992 and served for 8 years as CEO of this 400-employee company. He was an Ernst & Young Entrepreneur of the Year in San Diego in 1999. From 2002–2009, Chris was CEO of Opportunity International, a Christian microfinance organization in 28 countries. In 2009, Chris cofounded Edify, which facilitates loans and training to 12,000 Christian schools that educate 3 million children living in poverty in developing nations. He was CEO for years. In 2022, he cofounded Ardent Mentoring, which matches high-capacity, Christian mentors with social entrepreneurs. Chris lives in San Diego and has been married to Jane for thirty-nine years. They have one wonderful son, Andrew.

LLOYD REEB is a successful real estate developer who cofounded the Halftime Institute in 1998 alongside his mentor, Bob Buford. It has grown into a global movement, helping thousands of highly successful leaders discover their purpose and experience deep joy in giving back in their second half of life. Lloyd has done thousands of keynotes over twenty-five years about building a 100x life, and he has invested more than twenty thousand hours in coaching high-capacity leaders who are building organizations to bring God's love and compassion to the deepest needs in the world. Lloyd and his wife, Linda, live in Charlotte, North Carolina, and have three married adult children and three grandchildren.

LIST OF RESOURCES

PREVIOUS BOOKS AUTHORED BY CHRISTOPHER A. CRANE

Makonen Getu, Christopher A. Crane, and Bettina Gomez-Garcia, *Pathway to Flourishing Godly Nations: Low-Fee Christian Schools for Children Living in Poverty* (self-pub., Edify, 2022).

Christopher A. Crane, *A Dream and a Coconut Tree: Transforming Education for the Poor* (self-pub., EMT Communications, LLC, 2019).

Christopher A. Crane and Mike Hamel, *Executive Influence: Impacting Your Workplace for Christ* (Colorado Springs: NavPress, 2003).

PREVIOUS BOOKS AUTHORED BY LLOYD REEB

Lloyd Reeb, *Finally Connected: Deep, Rewarding Relationships in Your Second Half* (self-pub., Halftime Institute, 2022).

Lloyd Reeb, *Halftime for Couples: Building a Second Half of Impact and Adventure Together* (self-pub., Halftime Institute, 2012).

Lloyd Reeb, *The Second Half: Real stories. Real adventures. Real significance.* (self-pub., Halftime Institute, 2008).

Lloyd Reeb and Bill Wellons, *Unlimited Partnership: Igniting a Marketplace Leader's Journey to Eternal Significance* (Nashville: B&H Books, 2007).

Lloyd Reeb, *From Success to Significance: When the Pursuit of Success Isn't Enough* (Grand Rapids: Zondervan, 2004).

Made in the USA
Monee, IL
09 February 2024

53233700R00125